THE ANATOMY C

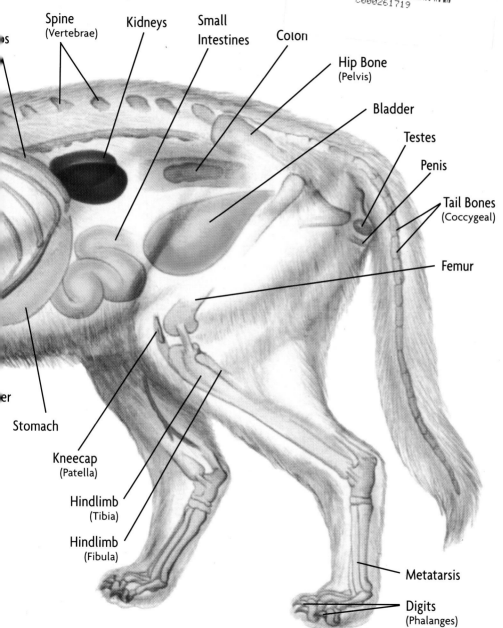

Bengal Cat

◇

By Dennis Kelsey-Wood

CONTENTS

PUBLISHED IN THE UNITED KINGDOM BY:

INTERPET
P U B L I S H I N G

Vincent Lane, Dorking   Surrey RH4 3YX   England

ISBN 1-84286-046-1

PHOTO CREDITS
Photography by Isabelle Francais, Cheryl Ertelt and Alan Robinson
with additional photographs by BJ Andrews, Michael W Brim,
Cat Fanciers Association, Carolina Biological Supply,
Fleabusters Rx for Fleas, James R Hayden, RBP, Interpet, Dwight R Kuhn,
Dr Dennis Kunkel, Jean S Mill, W P Mara, Jeff Michals, Pet Profiles,
Phototake, Jean Claude Revy, Erin Winters and WB Saunders Company.

The publisher wishes to thank the following owners, whose cats appear in
this book: Barbara J Andrews, Andrew De Prisco, Jaime Gardner, James
Lambri, Jeanne A Lee, Charles and Mary McGee and Jean S Mill.

BENGAL CAT

From the very beginnings of the cat fancy, there have always been spotted cats in evidence. These trace back to the original wild cats that were domesticated in the land of the pharaohs about 4000 years ago. The tabby pattern from which they were developed is still pre-eminent in street cats throughout the world. However, from the viewpoint of 19th-century cat breeders, the problem with spotted cats was they could be seen in any town or village. Breeders wanted more exotic types on which to build the then new feline hobby.

This need was met with the Persian and Siamese breeds, which quickly began to dominate the cat fancy. In their wake, other exotic breeds followed and spotted cats went into decline. For many years, the spotted British Shorthair, and the breeds to which the pattern was transferred, remained the only cats of this beautiful pattern in the hobby.

THE WINDS OF CHANGE

By the 1950s, things were beginning to change and there was a growing interest in spotted cats.

The Egyptian Mau was developed. It was to be followed by the Oriental Spotted Tabby, the Ocicat and the California Spangled. However, as pretty as these breeds were, they failed to fully meet the growing need for a cat having spots of true leopard-like type. The problem was that the domestic cat's ancestors (*Felis sylvestris* in its many subspecific forms) never had that type of rosette or arrowhead coat pattern.

A cross between a domestic cat and an appropriately patterned wild cat was needed. This was achieved under captive conditions (and it also happens in the wild) but no one was ever able to develop these hybrids beyond the first generation. That was until Jean Sugden of California arrived on the scene. By chance, Jean produced a hybrid from the needed wild cat/domestic cross. She was convinced that a domestic cat with a leopard-like coat was feasible.

Against this backdrop follows the story of how feasibility became a reality. It resulted in the Bengal cat breed. Not only has it become a top breed in Britain but

A Bengal is a cat that resulted from a cross between a domestic cat and a wild felid. The pure-bred Bengal must be at least three generations removed from the initial hybridisation.

it has also achieved this in a relatively short period of time. It ended the last millennium as being one of its most remarkable, as well as unusual, successes.

Today the breed is seen throughout the world and continues to gain devotees with each passing year. Without doubt the Bengal represents a major milestone in the feline hobby. It is one the most important breeds ever to have been developed.

WHAT IS A BENGAL?

A Bengal is a cat at least three generations removed from a hybrid of a wild felid crossed with a domestic cat. The resulting offspring of the original mating were judiciously back-crossed to domestic cats. Until at least the fourth generation has been achieved without a wild cat in its pedigree, the hybrids are called foundation cats or Bengal variants. In some associations, a fifth generation is required before the foundation hybrids can be called Bengals.

Only when the hybrids have reached this stage are they eligible as full exhibition felines. Also, only full Bengal cats are regarded as being fully domesticated and suitable as household pets. These have the gentle disposition of a domestic cat, combined with the coat pattern and colour, as well as some of the non-dangerous traits, of a truly wild species.

THE CRYSTAL PALACE SHOW

On 13 July 1871, an event took place that changed the world of the domestic cat. In the Crystal Palace at Sydenham, London, the world's first all-breed cat show took place. It was organised by Harrison Weir (1824–1906), a noted animal artist and great lover of British Shorthairs.

The success of the cat show saw Weir become a noted cat judge and author. Today he is regarded as the 'father of the cat fancy.' In his later years he complained that Eastern cats were causing the demise of his beloved British Shorthairs. This did not endear him to Persian owners, whose cats were now beginning to dominate the hobby.

The Crystal Palace show attracted thousands of people, many of whom had never seen, or were not even aware of, some of the breed types. On display were many British Shorthairs, Siamese, Manx and a wild cat. Also present was a cat reputed to be direct from Persia. It was said to have a delightful personality and its colour was black, grey and white. White Persians were also on view. For many visitors these were by far the most impressive exhibits, with their pale blue eyes and flowing fur.

Originally the Bengal was a spotted-only breed. Today the classic tabby pattern, in a modified form, has been transferred to it under the name of marbled in order to create an alternative variety. The original colours are also being added to, though many of these have not as yet gained official recognition. These changes to the original concept of the breed's pattern and colour are par for the course in the cat fancy but are not appreciated by all devotees.

THE ASIAN LEOPARD CAT

The wild species used by Jean S Mill in her breeding programme has the common name of Asian leopard cat (Alc) or simply leopard cat. Its full scientific name is *Felis bengalensis*

Examples of the F^1 generation, queens bred by Jean Mill.

THE F GENERATIONS
The offspring of the wild parental generation are known as being F^1 cats. When mated back to a domestic cat, the result is the F^2 generation. When these are paired to a domestic cat, the F^3 generation is produced. While many cats of the F^1 through F^3 generations have sound temperaments, others may be less reliable. The general recommendation is that cats up to F^3 are best suited to only highly experienced cat owners and breeders. It was found that by the F^4 generation, the cats had become as reliable in their nature as any domestic cat. It is this generation that is regarded as being fully domesticated and suited to any potential pet owner.

bengalensis, this being what is called the nominate form (the type on which the species is based). R Kerr gave this name to it in 1792. He identified it from one he caught after seeing it swimming in the Bay of Bengal.

However, in more recent taxonomic listings, the name *Prionailurus bengalensis bengalensis*, first used by Pocock in 1917, is the preferred name for many zoologists. Either of these is correct. There are numerous subspecies, such as the Amur leopard cat, *Felis bengalensis euptilura*.

The leopard cat is one of 37 wild cats and is distributed

throughout Asia from Afghanistan to China and Siberia, as well as numerous Asiatic islands. In all, Jean has used four leopard cats to create different breeding lines. About six or so other leopard cats are also thought to have been used by others in helping create the breed's present wild-cat gene pool. Although more populous than most wild cats, leopard cats are nonetheless classed as endangered across most of their range.

The leopard cat is a most beautiful feline with a size and weight of 3.2–6.8 kgs (7–15 lbs), which approximates that of the domestic cat. Its head and body length is 44–107 cms (17.6–43 ins) plus a tail of 23–44 cms (9–17.3 ins). Its coat varies considerably according to subspecies. In tropical countries it is a pale yellow to tawny brown, while in colder regions it is more of a grey or grey-brown. The underparts are cream to white.

The base colour, including the underparts, is dotted with dark brown or black solid spots or arrowhead markings. Alternatively, there may be rosettes, which have a light coloured centre. The tail is banded with black. The fur is short, dense and soft to the touch. Eye colour is yellow-brown to greenish yellow.

The head is medium to small and the ears are medium to large. The rear of each ear is black with

One of the types of Asian leopard cats used in the development of the Bengal. This photograph was taken in Belize by breeder BJ Andrews.

a conspicuous white centre. Two dark bands are seen on either side of a thin medium broken band that runs over the crown to the back of the neck. The head, when viewed from the front, has a longer, less round appearance than that seen in most wild species. The eyes are quite prominent, as befits a nocturnal creature. However, the leopard cat may be active during daylight, depending on the type of terrain in which it lives.

The main food of these cats is rodents, but they will also take any reptile, bird or mammal that they are capable of overpowering. They live in a variety of habitats; these include tropical rainforests, open country and coniferous forests in the colder parts of their range. They are partially arboreal (tree-dwelling) and excellent swimmers. They are considerably more agile than domestic cats.

Leopard cats appear to be less disturbed by the proximity of humans than most other wild felids, indeed breeding, at times, in coffee and other plantations. This fact has certainly made it easier to breed from them, but this by no means diminishes that achievement. These cats have lived in excess of 13 years under captive conditions.

THE FIRST CHANCE BREEDING
During 1963 Jean Sugden (Mill) acquired a female leopard cat. It was kept at her then home in Yuma, Arizona. Feeling that it might be lonely, Jean introduced it to a black domestic cat, which was to act as a companion. It was not thought a mating between the two was possible. But it was, and a female named Kin Kin resulted. She in turn produced offspring. The unfortunate death of Jean's husband in 1965 brought to an end this breeding programme. But it had fired the idea in Jean's mind of what might be accomplished should time and events prove more favourable. There are no surviving cats from the initial programme.

THE BREED BEGINS
In 1975, Jean remarried to become Jean Mill. She moved to Covina, California. There she built spacious 10 x 10-foot cages in

WHAT'S IN A NAME?
The leopard cat is known in different countries by the following names: in France, *chat leopard du Bengale*; in Spain, *gato Bengali*; in Germany, *Bengalkatze*; in Russia, *koshka Amurskii kot Bengalskaya*; in India, *chita billi, huli bekku* and *wagati*; in Thailand, *maew dao*; in Myanmar (Burma), *kye thit* or *thit kyuk* and in China, *bao mao, shih hu, shan mao* and *jin chien mao*.

All modern Bengals derive from the cats used by Jean Mill in her second experimental programme to produce the new 'leopard cat.'

order to put in hand her second breeding programme. Her new husband Bob was allergic to cats and this made it necessary to house the felines outdoors.

At about this time, Jean met Dr Willard Centerwall. He was involved in a genetic research programme to try and understand the reason for the leopard cat's partial immunity to feline leukaemia, a major disease in domestic cats. In the course of the programme, leopard cat hybrids were produced. These became surplus to Dr Centerwall's needs once blood samples had been taken from them.

Jean acquired eight of these individuals. Not all of these cats were to be used in Jean's Millwood cattery programme, as it was called. Some produced no live births, one had only small sterile males and several ate their kittens at birth. These instances underscore just a few of the problems and frustrations that were met. Only 'Pennybank' and 'Praline' appear in modern Millwood pedigrees.

HYBRID PROBLEMS

The greatest difficulty to be met when attempting to transfer given genes from one species to another is that the genes involved are rarely linked in favourable ways. As desirable genes are transferred, there will always be undesirables being transferred with them. Another problem that became manifest was that F^1 generation males ('F' meaning 'filial,' from the Latin for sons or daughters) were sterile.

This was also often the case in the F^2, and even in some F^3 individuals. This meant that normal F^1, F^2 and F^3 interbreeding was not possible. Back-crossing and outcrossing had to take place to create each new generation. It was also found that while many of the F^1 offspring closely resembled their wild parent, a desirable hope, their temperament, from a domestic standpoint, left much to be desired.

Matters improved considerably in the F^2 and F^3 generations in respect to this trait, but regression was evident in respect of the desired coat quality and pattern. As a result, back-crosses to an original wild parent were required. Genetically, this created a new parental generation from which new F^1 and F^2 families would be developed. The objective was to create a more favourable mix of genes. These numerous delays meant that developing this unique breed was a long and difficult process.

Yet another genetic problem was that many of the genes for colour and pattern in domestic cats are carried in what is known as a recessive manner. They are not evident when in a single dose. Such genes were transferred from domestic cats to the hybrid generations of the developing Bengal breed. As a consequence, they were eventually able to double up and become evident. Once identified, many of the individuals carrying the double dose had to be

removed from the breeding pool. With much resolve, and no doubt with many tears of disappointment, the problems were eventually overcome to a large degree. The Bengal is testimony to that dedication.

BREED RECOGNITION

The first 'leopard cats' ever registered were under that name with the Cat Fanciers Association (CFA) of America in 1982. Jean Mill owned one of these. However, no further registrations were made in the following years with that registry. It was to be with The International Cat Association (TICA) of America (formed in 1979) that the breed was to gain international recognition, commencing with registrations made in 1983.

By 1985 Jean had produced a number of exciting F^2 and F^3 individuals. These were displayed in TICA 'Exhibition Only' classes. They were always the centre of much attention from breeders and the public alike. By this means, and numerous articles in magazines, the breed's fame began to spread. TICA granted the Bengal championship show status in 1991. The creation of The International Bengal Cat Society was another most influential means by which the breed gained valuable promotion. It remains the breed's premier club to this day.

THE FIRST STANDARD

When Jean was required to produce the first breed standard, it is interesting to note she initially submitted data only for the coat colour, length and pattern. The pattern was allocated 50%, colour 40% and length 10% of her points. However, Jean was advised by TICA that a breed could not be based so narrowly. Conformational aspects now had

The coat of the Bengal was the main focus of the first standard, in which all of the allocated points were given to the various aspects of the coat.

to be considered.

The breed was still in its infancy, and as the coat was the key feature of the breed, it was extremely difficult for the founder to decide on matters of conformation. Jean was acutely aware of the problems that could ensue if undue importance was applied to anatomical parts. If the word 'long' for muzzle length was used, this could no doubt result in Bengals with a muzzle looking more befitting of a Greyhound than a leopard cat! If 'short' was the choice, this could result in Bengals that had a face looking somewhat like that of an Exotic Shorthair.

In all instances, the founder therefore attempted to take the 'medium' path. She felt that the finer points could be adjusted at a later date once the crucial, and difficult to retain, leopard cat coat genes had become well established within the breed's genetic pool. Her standard was adopted by TICA. In the following years, the Bengal gained recognition

OBNOXIOUS DOMESTIC CATS

Any domestic cat is capable of biting and scratching if not correctly bred, reared and cared for. If a Siamese, a British Shorthair or other breed is decidedly unfriendly, it is regarded as being an obnoxious, thus untypical, example of its breed. But if a Bengal displays the same nature, it becomes a case of 'it's the wild cat genes coming to the fore.'

The truth is that if a Bengal is less than perfect in its temperament, it is infinitely more probable, genetically, that its unfriendly nature was derived from one or more of its domestic ancestors than from that of its distant wild relatives. Bengal breeders have always been aware of the need to ensure that the breed is better than most others for this trait. It can be truthfully stated that at this time Bengal breeders pay greater attention to temperament than does the average cat breeder.

with one association after the other. The original TICA standard became the blueprint on which all others were based.

THE BREED IN BRITAIN

From the British perspective, the Bengal first appeared in the country around 1990 or 1991. The Governing Council of the Cat Fancy (GCCF), Britain's largest registry, gave the breed preliminary recognition in 1997, having accepted the breed for registration in 1992. In 1998, the Federation Internationale Feline (FIFe), a major world association of cat clubs, also recognised the breed. The Cat Association (CA), the second of Britain's registries, is the British representative of FIFe.

In 1992 just 61 Bengals were registered with the GCCF. In each

The Oriental Shorthair may have been used to create the Bengal.

DOMESTIC CATS USED

A number of domestic breeds had been used in the development stages of the Bengal breed and these include the Egyptian Mau, Ocicat, Abyssinian, Burmese, Siamese and various domestic shorthairs of unknown ancestry. During a visit by the Mills to India in 1980, a domestic shorthair, later named Millwood Tory of Delhi, was acquired. He had a profound impact on the breed's development. He is seen on many of the early pedigrees. His coat very much resembled that of the leopard cat. It is speculated that it was from Tory that the glitter factor (a gold or pearl dusting to the tips of the hairs) might have been derived.

Tory was registered with the Cat Fanciers Association (CFA) as both a domestic shorthair and, under the name of Millwood Tory of Delhi, as an Indian Mau. He was used successfully by Egyptian Mau breeders at a time when their bloodlines needed rejuvenation. He was therefore unusual in having played a major role in two separate breeds.

of the following six years the annual number of registrations increased. By 1998 the number had risen to 1,510. This made the breed the sixth most popular cat in Britain. Attaining its present level of popularity must be regarded as a spectacular achievement in such a short time. Given

A blue-eyed, snow-spotted Bengal, representing one of the many attractive colour patterns in the modern breed.

this fact, the Bengal may yet confound the odds and continue to climb even higher up the registration table.

THE FUTURE
Over the coming years, the Bengal will no doubt establish itself as the obvious choice for those wanting a spotted feline having wild cat genes in its not-too-distant ancestry. However, the price to pay for popularity in any cat breed is that it becomes the focus of those who see it as an opportunity to widen the original colour range and even to introduce new hair types.

This will be an especially difficult problem for the Bengal. It is not a typical cat breed. Its very essence is that the genes that have been retained from the leopard cat are unique within domestic felines. They are very precious and can easily be lost if not managed with great care.

During the breed's development years, Jean Mill, and many of the other pioneer breeders, devoted much effort to neutering, and selling as pets, cats displaying the very genes which some are now trying to establish as acceptable breed varieties. They were regarded as unwanted genetic material not conducive to helping retain and develop the leopard cat genes for the various types of spotting, as well as for the quality and colour of the coat.

The addition of new leopard cat colours or hair types into the Bengal gene pool can only dilute the very genes upon which the breed was originally created. Present and future breeders and owners must ponder carefully whether such additions are needed.

Will they be regarded at a future time as having caused this wonderful breed to go into regression? The problem will be that once the Bengal is swamped with an array of recessive genes for more colours, it will become impossible to maintain lines that are free of these. For the Bengal, the future holds both great expectations and more than a few problems to be overcome along the way. In the meantime, it remains a truly promising breed.

The marbled coat pattern results from the varied gene pool that has been employed in the breeding of modern Bengals.

Portrait of the

BENGAL CAT

Whether in its spotted or marbled coat pattern, a well-marked Bengal is a most alluring feline. The initial impression should be of a very alert cat with a muscular conformation and a very friendly disposition. The Bengal is a relatively large breed and should emanate more than a suggestion of a truly wild species of imposing stature.

The ultimate guide to the breed's description of conformation, patterns and colours is its standard of points. A breed club drafts this. It is then presented to a national registration authority of a given country for approval. When this is given, it is applied by judges at shows run under the rules of that particular association. While all breed standards are broadly similar in their requirements and list of breed faults, they may differ in detail, and accepted colours, from one association to another.

The following Bengal description is not that of any one association. It was prepared after reference to numerous standards. It will meet the needs of most pet owners. Those wishing to exhibit or breed should obtain the official standard of points of the associa-

FUZZIES

This term refers to the changes that may be displayed in a Bengal's coat pattern as it goes through different stages of its life. When a kitten is only a few weeks old, its spots or marbling can be very distinct from the ground colour. By 12 weeks of age, the pattern may begin to look very fuzzy. With the passage of more weeks (or months), it begins to regain its original quality.

However, some kittens never regain the beautiful markings they previously displayed. Still others may become fuzzy when they are two to three years old. This reality is obviously unfortunate but is a fact of life applicable, in different ways, within most cat breeds. Buyers should proceed by ensuring a kitten is from adults that display excellent patterns. They should also have a proven record of producing similar quality in their offspring.

GLITTER

This term refers to a feature of the hairs unique to the Bengal breed at this time. It is not, as yet, fully understood in respect of its genetics. It is described as being a gold or pearl dusting to the tips of the hairs depending on whether it is seen in the tabby or snow colours. It is created by each hair's having a translucent tip surrounding a reduced amount of pigment. Under certain light, the colour is refracted through the clear tip, which intensifies it. The contrast between this effect and the rest of the hair shaft gives the illusion of dusting or having a satin-like sheen.

It is thought that glitter is the result of a recessive mutation (gl) introduced very early into the Bengal breed by a domestic shorthair. It has been found that the extent of glitter varies according to the coat texture and is seen best on the shorter velvet-type coats. It also varies in its extent along the hair shaft. Jean Mill states, 'there seem to be degrees of expression implying that there are several if not many modifiers or blends.'

Whether or not glitter should be included within official Bengal standards has been the subject of debate. It is not mentioned in American standards but is included in that of the GCCF under the term 'dusting.' Those opposed to its inclusion point out that this factor was not inherited from the leopard cat and is not evident in all Bengals. To include it within a standard therefore may imply that its non-presence could result in an exhibit being at a disadvantage to an individual displaying the feature. This would be unfortunate from a breeding perspective.

The Bengal head appears as a medium wedge, with more rounded contours than the Oriental breeds.

tion with which their cats are registered.

Additional comments have been included where it was felt these would be beneficial to a better understanding of the description. Reference to American standards has importance to European owners. A number of American registries, such as TICA and the CFA, is now establishing themselves in Europe.

A standard can never be more than a basic guide to a breed. As such, it is open to considerable interpretation by breeders and judges. The only way a novice can fully appreciate a standard is to visit a number of cat shows. The winning exhibits can then be compared to the standard. The finer points can also be discussed with both judges and successful exhibitors.

DESCRIPTION OF THE BENGAL

Head: When looked at from above, this is a medium wedge that displays rounded contours rather than the straight lines seen in Oriental breeds. The head is longer than it is wide and high cheek bones are evident. The muzzle is well developed and round, with pronounced whisker pads and a firm chin. The nose should be large and broad and display a slightly puffed nose leather. Allowance must be made for jowls in mature males.

In profile, the head and muzzle again have a wedge appearance but with a gentle curve from the forehead to the

A UNIQUE CHARACTER

The Bengal character is the sum total of all the genes the cat has inherited from its many domestic-breed ancestors, plus those few genes that have been retained from its leopard cat ancestor. Given the wide mix of breeds used in developing the Bengal, it is obvious its character will be strongly influenced by those breeds most commonly found in its background.

As such it will, as a breed, tend to exhibit a wider ranger of traits than would most other breeds that have been bred for countless generations within a closed gene pool nucleus. The Bengal ancestors include the Burmese, Abyssinian, Ocicat, Mau, Siamese and various domestic cats, both short- and longhaired.

The general features common to most of these ancestors are being athletic, intelligent, often quite vocal, very energetic, extremely loving and often demanding of their owner's attentions. In the case of the Bengal, it can be added that it, more often than most breeds, exhibits a fascination for water. However, this may not extend to actually swimming as it does to its leopard cat ancestors.

It will paw at still water so as to clear any dust from its surface, as would the wild cat before it drinks from a river or stream. Some Bengals will splash about in shallow water and even under showers. With this in mind, owners should ensure such water is never hot. Always keep toilet lids closed to avoid the risk that a young Bengal might reach into the water and accidentally fall in. Aquariums in the home without hoods should be covered, or they may end up without fish in them!

The eyes should appear oval and be coloured to complement the coat colour.

bridge of the nose. The nose in profile displays a very slight concave curve. Overall, the head is of medium to small size when compared to body size. However, breeders should not seek smallness as an extreme feature, which would be incorrect. The neck should be thick and muscular but proportionate to body size. If the head is an ideal size, the neck will look somewhat large.

Ears: The ears should be medium to small in size with a wide base opening and rounded tips. The ears broadly follow the contours of the head and are set as much on the side of the head as on its top. They display a slight forward tilt when viewed in profile. Some furnishings (hairs at the open base

and on the ear tips) are acceptable, but these should never be excessive nor appear as lynx-like tufts at the extremity of the ears.

Eyes: The eyes should be oval, though they may appear slightly almond-shaped. Large without being unduly bold, they are set on a slight inclination as though pointing towards the ear base. The eye colour is variable with each variety.

Body: The body should be long and substantial, displaying ample muscle, especially in males. The hindquarters are slightly higher than are the shoulders. Body size is large without being either as heavy or tall as the biggest of the domestic breeds. Typical weight range is 4.5–5.5 kgs (10–12 lbs) for a female and about 6.5–8.25 kgs (14–18 lbs) for a male, though some individuals may be heavier.

Legs & Paws: Legs should be medium in length. The rear legs are longer than those at the front. Bone should be substantial as befits a cat with considerable climbing and jumping capabilities. The paws are large and round.

Tail: The tail should be medium to long, thick and even, though it may be slightly tapered towards its rounded tip.

Coat: Of short to medium length, the coat, often called a pelt in this breed, should be very dense and extremely soft and plush to the touch. Allowance should be made for a slightly longer coat in kittens.

Breed Faults: Apart from general faults that apply to all cat breeds (genetic and anatomical defects), the following are specific faults within the Bengal breed: aggressive behaviour (the most serious fault), Oriental head or body type, cobby body or that which is similar to the Abyssinian or Burmese breeds, overly long and rough or coarse coat, ticked coat, tail tip the wrong colour, whip-like tail, incorrect paw pad colour, lack of spotting on the belly (except in blue-eyed snow

kittens), white patches of fur other than the ocelli (the spots on the back of the ears).

Temperament: This forms part of American standards but not those of the GCCF and Bengal Cat Club of Britain. Temperament must be unchallenging, and any sign of aggressive behaviour will result in disqualification of a show cat. A cat may display signs of fear and shyness. It may vocally complain and seek to avoid human contact, but must never threaten to strike out at or bite any person.

COAT PATTERNS

There are two basic coat patterns seen in the Bengal, spotted and the marbled. Each of these is available in two colours, brown or snow. The snow colours are seen in either blue-eyed or any-other-colour-eyed (AOC). There are thus six Bengal varieties.

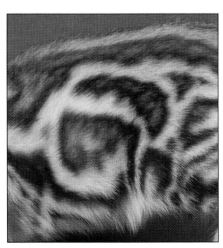

The spotted pattern should be clearly defined, as on this brown-spotted cat.

Spotted Pattern: This is the pattern for which the breed was created and remains the most popular at this time, especially in its rosetted form. Head, neck, legs, feet and tail markings are the same for both spotted and marbled varieties. The eyes are circled with dark rims. Ideally, these will connect to vertical lines that extend over the head and down the neck, where they may break up and become rosettes on the shoulders. On the forehead, a tabby 'M' mark is seen. This connects to a number of often broken lines that go over the head and down the neck. From the lower eyelids, two dark mascara lines extend over the cheeks.

The neck carries dark necklets, which extend to the shoulders. Dark chin straps are desirable. The legs are banded with complete or broken stripes, which become blotches or spots on the feet. The tail is banded with rings. These may be complete, broken or spotted. The tail must display a dark-coloured tip.

The body is covered with spots. These may form rosettes, arrowhead markings or blotches. These must be scattered over the coat in a random or horizontal manner. Vertically aligned spots are a fault as they are indicative of the mackerel tabby pattern. The stomach must be spotted other than in the kittens of blue-eyed snows.

A Bengal kitten, showing the wild colouring so desirable to many advocates of the Bengal breed.

It is preferred that the spots be as large as possible. They may form rosettes in which one or two spots form a part circle surrounding a centre that is of a distinctly lighter colour. Rosettes are especially attractive, giving a real leopard-like look to the coat, but they are not essential. Arrowhead markings where the point faces the rear of the body are very desirable and characteristic of the wild leopard cat. The contrast between the ground colour and the spots should be as a great as possible in order to give the spots a distinctive outline.

Marbled Pattern: This pattern differs from the spotted in respect to the markings on the body. This said, the marbling effect might also be seen on the tail, which may or may not additionally display spotting and rings. The pattern was derived from the classic (also known as blotched) tabby pattern seen in domestic breeds. It is not a pattern seen in the wild leopard cat. However, it appeared early in the development stages of the Bengal and has proved to be very popular.

Marbling is created by the effect of the leopard pattern genes on the classic tabby. In an excellent example, the result is a strikingly beautiful pelt-like coat. While not quite a mirror of the marbling seen in wild cats, it is nonetheless as close as has yet been achieved in a domestic breed; as such, it is unique to the Bengal.

The pattern comprises large swirled patches or streaks. These must not be symmetrical and they should suggest an horizontal flow. They should not form the bull's eye or oyster shape seen in the classic tabby. Parts of the marbled pattern, especially on the back, may break up into what is called chain marbling. The effect is stunning and gives the coat a wild cat look similar to that seen is such species as the ocelot, margay and especially the clouded leopard.

Colours

Brown Tabby: This refers to the ground colour. It may be any variety of light- to mid-brown. However, yellow, buff, golden or orange displaying plenty of rufism is preferred. Rufism is a term used to describe the polygenes that create a richer shade of yellow to brown and red. Compare the ginger of a typical moggie with the rich red of an exhibition cat— it is rufous genes that create the difference. The ground may also be a grey colour, which should not be penalised.

Spots or marbling will be black or various shades of brown. The more contrast there is between the spots and the ground colour, the better. A light-coloured spot, called an ocellus, on the

The blue-eyed snow-spotted pattern appears diluted, as it has a cream or ivory ground colour.

back of the ear is desirable, though its absence is not a fault. The whisker pads and chin should ideally be white, though a very pale colour is acceptable.

The throat, chest and underparts should be white or a pale colour, this also being applicable to the inner parts of the legs. White or light-coloured spectacles should surround the dark rims of the eyes. The nose and lips are edged in black while the centre of the nose should be brick red. The paw pads must be black.

In the marbled pattern, it is preferred that three or more colours are seen. These will comprise the ground colour, the marbling itself and a darker edging to this. Extra colour will be in the form of a more intense rufous effect on the ground colour around the marbling. In both the spotted and marbled patterns of the brown tabby, the standard of the GCCF states that the overall impression of the coat is one of being dusted with gold (known as glitter). Eye colour is green, gold or hazel, with deeper shades being the most desirable.

Blue-Eyed Snow: This colour is more correctly called a colour pattern. It appeared early in the Bengal's development as a consequence of recessive genes for what is genetically known as the Siamese colour restriction. These genes were inherited from the domestic cats, not from the leopard cat. Like the marbled pattern, it has proved extremely popular. On this account, it was specifically bred for as a variety.

The effect of the pattern is that pigmentation is diluted. The ground colour becomes a cream or ivory colour. The point markings (face, ears, legs and tail) are a darker colour than that of the body markings, though minimal contrast is preferred. The pattern colour ranges from charcoal to light or dark brown. Paw pads are a dark rosy brown. In America this pattern is called the seal lynx point. Eye colour is blue.

AOC-Eyed Snow: This colour pattern is derived from either the Burmese or Tonkinese colour restrictions. The Burmese restriction is darker than the Siamese. The Tonkinese is the result of an individual's inheriting a Siamese restriction gene from one parent and a Burmese gene from the other.

The effect is a midway point between the Siamese and Burmese restrictions. The genes do not blend as might be thought. It is a case that the darker Burmese restriction is incompletely dominant over the lighter Siamese gene. In America these varieties are officially classed as being seal sepia tabby (Burmese restriction) or seal mink tabby (Tonkinese restriction).

The ground colour is ivory to tan. The pattern will range from charcoal to light or dark brown. Eye colour is gold, green or blue-green. The gold eye colour is inherited from the Burmese, the green and blue-green from the Tonkinese. In both the blue-eyed and the AOC-eyed standards of the GCCF, it states that the coat should give the appearance of having a pearl-like dusting (glitter).

Other Colours and Varieties

The Bengal, as a breed, may carry within its genetic pool every recessive gene colour and pattern existing in domestic cats. While most breeders, the traditionalists, will select against these variants in their breeding programmes,

Showing the range of colour patterns in the breed, here are a blue-eyed marbled snow and a brown marbled Bengal.

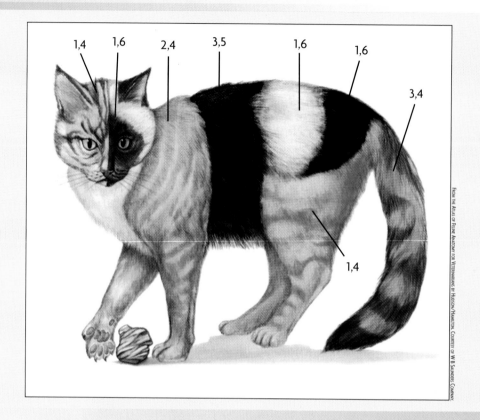

1,4   1,6   2,4   3,5   1,6   1,6   3,4   1,4

From the Atlas of Feline Anatomy for Veterinarians by Hudson/Hamilton, Courtesy of W B Saunders Company.

PARTICOLOURED CAT

Not a new breed of feline, this 'particoloured cat' illustrates the many possibilities of the feline coat. Since cats come in three basic hair lengths, short, long and rex (curly), all three coat lengths are illustrated here. Additionally, different coat patterns, such as mackerel tabby, Abyssinian and self-coloured, are depicted to demonstrate the differences.

1–3   COAT TYPES
1 Shorthair coat
2 Rex (curly) coat
3 Longhair coat

4–6   COAT COLOUR PATTERNS
4 Mackerel (tabby)
5 Abyssinian
6 Self-coloured

SKIN AND HAIRCOAT OF CATS

Schematic illustration of histologic layers of the integument skin.

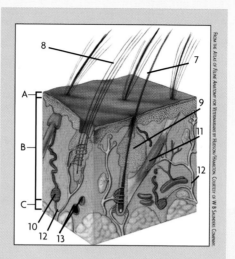

A Epidermis
B Dermis
C Subcutis

7 Primary hair
8 Secondary hairs
9 Area of sebaceous gland
10 Apocrine sweat gland
11 M arrector pili
12 Nerve fibre
13 Cutaneous vessels
14 Tactile hair
15 Fibrous capsule
16 Venous sinus
17 Sensory nerve fibres
18 External root sheath
19 Hair papilla

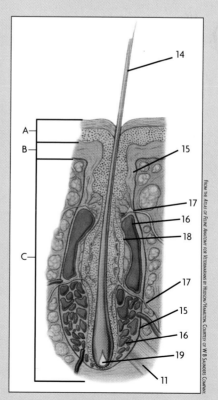

Schematic illustration of a tactile hair (whisker).

FROM THE ATLAS OF FELINE ANATOMY FOR VETERINARIANS BY HUDSON/HAMILTON. COURTESY OF W B SAUNDERS COMPANY.

FROM THE ATLAS OF FELINE ANATOMY FOR VETERINARIANS BY HUDSON/HAMILTON. COURTESY OF W B SAUNDERS COMPANY.

Many softer patterns have emerged in the modern Bengal, which are not as dramatic as the darker spotted patterns.

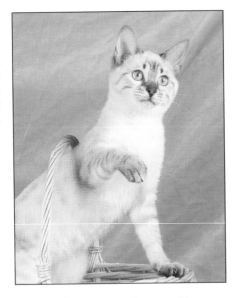

type variety.

Generally, the reason for retaining or introducing non-recognised colours is financial. If the colour or variation proves popular, those establishing it are obviously in a head-start position. If it ultimately gains official recognition, its breeders will gain even greater status. If a given colour fails to gain recognition, its devotees may change tack, give the variation its own name and develop it as being a new cat breed. If the colour pattern or hair type fails to attract sufficient followers, then it simply fades into obscurity. This is the way the cat fancy has always developed.

Presently, the following variants are known to exist in the Bengal breed. The blue variant is gaining more followers and may one day be accepted as an official variety. It is more a grey than a true blue. The silver is a variation that will no doubt gain in popularity as it can often be quite striking. The smoke, where the underfur is white or cream and the rest of the hair shaft is pigmented, is another of the present variations. The black in its non-agouti form will show faint tabby spotting. The gene creating it is the same as that which creates the black leopard or so-called panther. The red, thus its linked variety, the tortoise-shell, is a dominant mutation that cannot be transmitted without its

Dark markings, in spots, rosettes or stripes, are desirable on the coat of the Bengal.

others, the progressives, will choose to deliberately establish certain of these. In some instances, genes may be deliber-ately introduced specifically to create a new colour or even hair-

The popularity of a breed determines its ultimate future, provided the breed doesn't fall into irresponsible hands. The Bengal has been enthusiastically received by fanciers around the world.

presence being obvious. In respect of hair types, longhaired individuals occasionally turn up in Bengal litters. They have no realistic value for onward progress.

Popularity, rather than any other factor, has a track record in the cat fancy for being the ultimate justification for eventual official recognition. Whether such a fickle factor is beneficial to this unique breed may be the source of considerable future controversy.

The Bengal is a beautiful, active and intelligent feline that promises to delight and enchant the smitten owner.

Purchasing a
BENGAL CAT

THE PURCHASING PROCESS

Never rush into the purchase of a companion that is to be given the freedom of your home and will become an integral part of your life. A pure-bred cat may live 20 or more years. This is a long time. It is very prudent to take all those steps that will minimise the chances of your ever regretting the choice you make. Once you have decided on the sex, age, reason for purchase (pet, show or breeding) and desired colour pattern, proceed cautiously, heeding all the advice given here. By following a planned process of selection, you will also gain much useful information.

Before the decision to purchase a Bengal is made, careful consideration should be given to the implications and responsibilities of cat ownership. If more owners would do this, there would be far fewer half-starved pets roaming our streets or having to live in local animal rescue centres.

OWNER RESPONSIBILITY

The initial cost of a Bengal represents only a fraction of its lifetime's cost. The first question is, 'Can you afford one?' The kitten needs vaccinations to protect it against various diseases. Boosters are then required every year. Cat food is more costly than that for dogs. There is also the cost of cat litter every week. Periodic vet checks and treatment for illness or accident must be allowed for. When holidays are taken, you may need to board the pet at a cattery.

From the outset there will be additional costs apart from that of the kitten. It will need a basket, carrying box, feeding vessels, grooming utensils, scratching post a few toys and maybe a collar. If you have any doubts at all about

being able to supply all these needs, it is best not to obtain a cat.

Other matters also need careful thought. If you are planning to have a family, will your love for the Bengal be maintained once a baby arrives? Cats are generally not a problem with family newcomers providing they are not ignored or treated as being a threat to the baby. Never purchase a kitten for a child unless you want one yourself. If you are elderly, it is only fair to consider what would happen to your cherished pet if it were to outlive you or if you were to become hospitalised for long periods.

It is most unfortunate that many people rush into the purchase of cats on an impulse. They then find they cannot cope if problems, and extra costs, ensue. Some lose interest in the pet once it matures past its kitten stage. The evidence of these realities is easily seen in the growing number of cats abandoned or taken to animal shelters every year. Invariably their owners will make feeble excuses for why the cat cannot be kept. But the bottom line is they did not stop to consider at the outset what responsible ownership entailed.

The Bengal's potential behaviour patterns are such that the breed is best suited to those wanting an active companion.

DOCUMENTATION

When you take delivery of your kitten, certain paperwork should come with it:

1. Three- to five-generation pedigree.
2. Breeder-signed registration application form or change of owner registration form. This assumes the breeder has registered stock. If they have not, the kitten cannot be registered at a later date. It is worth less than the kitten with registration paperwork. You are not recommended to purchase a kitten from unregistered parents.
3. Certificates of health, vaccination and neutering, if this has been effected. Ideally, it is desirable that the kitten's parents have been tested negative for major diseases. Additionally, the breeder should know the blood group of your kitten. This may be of importance at a later date.
4. Details of worming or other treatments attended.
5. Diet sheet, feeding timetable and brand names of food items used. This diet should be maintained for at least ten days while the kitten adjusts to the trauma of moving home.
6. Signed receipt for monies paid.
7. Signed copy of any guarantees. Not all breeders give a guarantee on the reasonable grounds that once the kitten leaves their care, its onward well-being is no longer under their control.

add up to a very mischievous feline on occasions. It is best to keep valuable fragile ornaments well clear of a Bengal. It loves to explore and paw at things as it does so.

However, when not in its hyperactive mood, it can be the epitome of a relaxed cat. It enjoys

TAKING KITTY HOME

Arrange collection of the kitten as early in the day as possible. If a long journey is involved, be sure to take a few breaks so kitty does not suffer from travel sickness. Do not make stops to show the kitten to friends; this represents a health hazard. Once home, offer the kitten a drink, then allow it to sleep if it so requires. Children must be educated to handle a kitten gently, never to tease it and to respect its sleeping privacy. Until it is litter-trained it should be restricted to the kitchen or another room with an easy-to-clean floor surface.

This is not a breed that likes to sit back and watch what is going on around it. Rather it wants to join in—or be the source of what's going on. It is a superb climber and great jumper, and is very inquisitive. This combination can nothing better than curling up or stretching out on or near its owner. It is a breed that comes complete with a wide range of vocalisations. Some of these may include sounds that are remnants of those used by its wild ancestor. As such, they are quite unique within domestic cat breeds. The Bengal will mix very well in a multi-pet household as long as duly supervised introductions are made.

There is little doubt that for many owners it is the breed's stunning looks that initially attract them to the Bengal. But it is its wonderful, and often very

Like any kitten, the Bengal toddler is curious and active, requiring careful supervision as it adjusts to life in its new home.

variable, patterns of behaviour that more often than not become the reason why a second Bengal is obtained.

BUYING A BENGAL

As a consequence of its endearing nature, the Bengal enjoys a wonderful reputation with cat judges. Many of these are on record as stating that the breed has a more reliable nature than do some of the long-established breeds. The advice is therefore this: If a Bengal is an F^4 or greater offspring (meaning F^5 and so on) it will be no more dangerous than any other cat breed. An F^4 offspring will have only one wild cat in its four-generation pedigree.

The first-time owner's best assurance that they are obtaining a true Bengal is to obtain the kitten from a member of the Bengal Cat Club, formed in 1993, or its equivalent in any other country. It must be registered with the GCCF or the Cat Association as a Bengal, or with an appropriate cat registry for cat owners living in other countries.

KITTEN OR ADULT?

Most potential owners normally want a kitten because it is so cute, cuddly and playful. A kitten is easily trained and has not yet developed bad habits, which the older Bengal may have done. This said, if you plan to breed or exhibit, there are advantages in obtaining a young adult. Other potential owners, such as the elderly, may benefit by avoiding the demanding needs of a young kitten. In both these instances, a good age is when the youngster is 9–15 months old. Even a fully mature Bengal may prove an excellent choice for some owners.

Kittens should not be obtained under 12 weeks old, though 14–16 weeks of age is better. No reputable breeder will sell them younger than this. Less caring breeders will let them go to new homes as young as eight weeks of age. Such juveniles will barely have been weaned. They will not have developed the needed resistance to major diseases. They are more likely to become stressed by the premature removal from their mother and siblings. Their vaccinations will not be fully effective. These facts will dramatically increase the risk of immediate problems.

SEX AND COLOUR PATTERN

If it is to be purely a pet, the Bengal's gender is unimportant. Both are delightful. Males are

usually larger, bolder and more outgoing. Females tend to be more discerning about which humans they like. However, each Bengal is an individual. Its character and health, more than its sex, should be the basis of selection. Again, the sex is unimportant for the potential exhibitor. It is not even necessary for the cat to be sexually 'entire.' Classes for neuters are offered in shows.

Those with breeding aspirations are advised to obtain only females. All pet owners should regard neutering (males) and spaying (females) as obligatory. Today this can be effected at any age after eight weeks.

The colour pattern is a matter of personal preference. It should never be placed ahead of health and character. Some colours and patterns will be more readily available than others will. The more popular varieties may be less costly than the rarer ones. This would generally not apply to prospective breeding or exhibition individuals where type quality will be as important as colour or pattern.

LOOK BEFORE YOU LEAP

It is important you view as many Bengal kittens as you can. This gives you a good mental picture of what an healthy typical example should look like and cost for the quality and colour you want. Normally, you will get what you

ADOPTING AN ADULT

Some owners, such as the elderly, may benefit by adopting an adult cat. They can avoid the demanding needs of a young kitten and enjoy the advantages of a well-trained adult, making grooming an easier task. Breeders and exhibitors can also benefit from purchasing an older cat because it is easier to assess the quality. Sometimes, though, older cats can have bad habits that are hard to break. So if you are thinking about obtaining an older cat, it is important to thoroughly investigate possible behavioural and health problems.

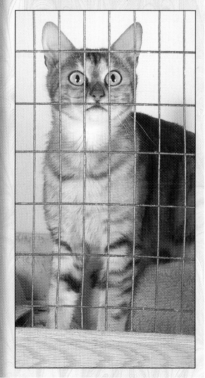

pay for. If you look for the cheapest kitten, there may be a sound reason why it is the cheapest!

The best place to start your search is a cat show. At these, most of the colour varieties will be on display. Purchase the show catalogue. It lists all the exhibitors and their addresses. You can see if any live in your immediate locality. Whenever possible, it is best to purchase locally so you can visit the home of the breeder. Some will insist you do so in order to be satisfied that you will make a good owner.

Shows and breeders are advertised in the various cat magazines available from newsagents. You can also contact a major cat registry. They will supply a list of national and regional clubs, which are usually able to supply breeder lists. When visiting a breeder, always make an appointment. Try to visit no more than one a day. This reduces the risk you may transport pathogens (disease-causing organisms) from one establishment to the next. Selecting a good breeder is a case of noting the environment in which the cats are kept, the attitude of the owner to you and their cats, and how friendly and healthy the kittens look. It is vital that the chosen kitty has an outgoing personality. It must not appear timid or very shy. This indicates a lack of breeder sociali-sation or a genetic weakness in its temperament. Either way, it is not a kitten you should select.

Selecting a Bengal kitten begins with finding a local breeder who can show you the queen along with the litter. Topspot Simba had only one kitten in her second litter, a female that was well socialised and wonderfully active. Breeders, Andrew De Prisco and BJ Andrews.

CHOOSING A KITTEN

If you choose the breeder wisely, and especially if a friend recommends him, this will limit the problems related to your making a poor choice. However, a little knowledge on what to look for will not go amiss. Observe the kittens from a distance to ensure none is unduly lethargic, which is never a good sign. If any display signs of illness, this should bring to an end any further thoughts of purchase from that source. A reputable breeder would not allow an ill kitten to remain within its litter.

It is always advisable to select a kitten that shows particular interest in you. Bengals are very discerning. If both of you are drawn to each other, this will greatly enhance the bonding essential for a strong relationship.

Once a particular kitten has been selected, it should be given a close physical inspection. The eyes and nose must show no signs of weeping or discharge. The ears will be erect and fresh smelling. The coat should look healthy, never dry and dull. There must be no signs of parasites in the fur. There will be no bald areas of fur, nor bodily swellings or abrasions. Lift the tail and inspect the anal region. This must be clean with no indication of congealed faecal matter. Any staining of the fur indicates current or recent diarrhoea.

AN HEALTHY KITTEN
Closely inspect any kitten before making a final decision. Keep in mind the following points:
Eyes and nose: Clean and clear with no signs of discharge.
Ears: Fresh-smelling and erect.
Coat: Healthy, not dull or dry.
Anal region: Clean with no staining of the fur.
Feet: Four toes on each foot, plus a dewclaw on the inside of each front leg.
Teeth: Correct bite.
There should be no signs of parasites or bald areas of fur. A potbelly may indicate worms.

The kitten must not display a potbelly. This may indicate worms or other internal disorders. Check the teeth to be sure of a correct bite. Bear in mind that

HOMEMADE TOYS

Cats love to play and pet shops have many cat toys to choose from. Sometimes, however, people give their cats homemade toys. These can be harmful to your cat, as they could have pieces that could break off and be swallowed. Only give your pet toys from the pet shop that have been proven safe for cats.

inside of each front leg.

With respect to the colour, there is no link between this and health in the Bengal. Any faults in the colour or its placement will only be of importance in breeding or exhibition individuals. The potential breeder/exhibitor should obtain a copy of the official standard so he is *au fait* with all colour, pattern, and body faults of the breed.

KITTY SHOPPING SPREE

Certain accessories should be regarded as obligatory and obtained before the kitten arrives at your home.

SCRATCHING POST

This will save the furniture from being abused! There are many models, some being simple posts, others are combined with play stations and sleeping quarters. These are preferred by active Bengals.

LITTER BOX(ES)

Some are open trays; others are domed to provide extra privacy. Still others have special bases in which odour removers are fitted.

CAT LITTER

There are numerous types on the market, each offering advantages and drawbacks. Avoid the low-cost types that contain a lot of dangerous dust. Use those that are fully biodegradable.

the jawbones do not develop at the same rate. Minor imperfections may correct themselves (they may also get worse) but major faults will not. Inspect the feet to see there are four toes on each, plus a dewclaw on the

FOOD/WATER DISHES

Polished metal has the longest wear life. Earthenware is less costly than metal and superior to the plastic types.

GROOMING TOOLS

These will comprise a good-quality bristle brush, a fine-toothed comb, nail trimmers and a soft chamois leather.

CAT COLLAR AND/OR HARNESS

Select elasticised collars. Be sure a name and address disc or barrel is fitted to this. A harness must be a snug but comfortable fit if it is to be effective.

CAT-CARRYING BOX

Essential for transporting the cat to the vet or other places, as well as for home restriction when needed. Be sure it is large enough to accommodate a fully-grown

CAT LITTER

The litter that is used in cat boxes can be very variable, and in many cases cats reject the use of a cat box because of the litter. Certainly, if your cat rejects the use of the cat box, you should try different litters. You can start with the litters available at your local pet shop, then you can try sand, dirt, cedar shavings or whatever will appeal to your cat. Several cat owners grow clover in a tray and their cats seem to prefer that. However, the tray is kept outdoors and the cats may simply be marking the clover tray rather than using it for elimination purposes.

Bengal, not just a kitten. The choice is between collapsible models, soft plastic types and, the best choice, those made of wood or fibreglass.

Before your kitten comes to its new home, be certain that you have acquired all of the necessary equipment and supplies.

Cat carriers are a necessity of cat ownership, though no cat welcomes the opportunity of being carted about in a crate. Nonetheless, the carrier is the only safe option for transport to the veterinary surgeon.

Double-bowl feeders are very convenient for feeding your cat. Go to your pet shop to purchase top-quality feeders, which should come in a variety of colours, styles and sizes.

There is nothing glamorous about purchasing a litter box, yet cat owners have few options in this regard. Consult your local pet shop to see a selection of boxes. Some cats do not accept a covered box, while others welcome the 'privacy.'

Liners are available for most litter trays to assist in keeping them clean and more manageable.

Purchasing a scratching post is a smart option for the cat owner. It's best to purchase a sturdy, well-made post that will last your cat years of utility.

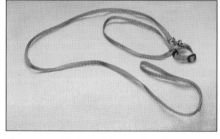

If you are considering walking your Bengal, you must have a lead that is suitable for a cat.

Your local pet shop should have an array of scratching posts that will delight your Bengal. Do not attempt to make a post yourself as many carpets are too weak to stand the tearing or may have been dyed with chemicals harmful to cats.

Your local pet shop should carry a full range of litter trays, litter boxes and the tools with which you keep the box clean.

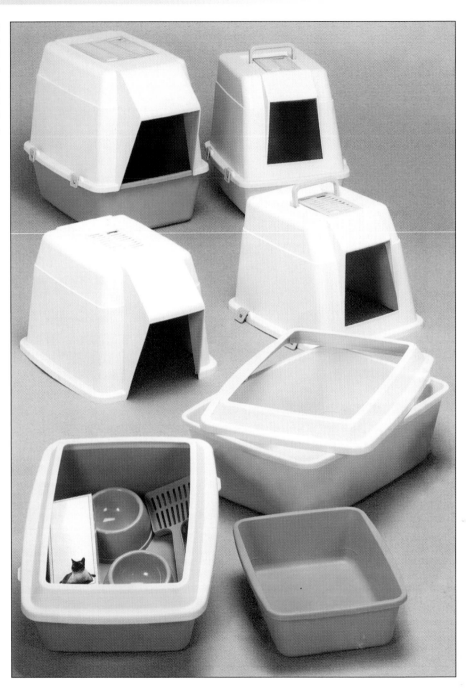

Cat toys are entertaining for cat and owner alike. Purchase toys that require interaction between you and your Bengal, thereby affording the cat exercise and companionship while playing.

Well-made scratching posts, constructed of strong hemp rope and wood, are preferred by cat owners. Posts with exercise stations are especially welcomed by the active Bengal.

Providing a Safe Home for Your ⸻
BENGAL CAT

For a kitten, its human environment holds many dangers. Its owner must protect it from these until it becomes agile and wiser. The following dangers lurk in typical households. Always check whether there are additional ones in your home. The most important decision you need to make from the outset is whether or not the kitten is to be given outdoor liberty.

HOW MUCH FREEDOM?
More than at any time in the past, the question of how much freedom a cat should be given is often the subject of heated debate. It is a very subjective matter. Here the more pertinent points are given so you can relate these to your home location. This, to a very large degree, should influence your decision.

Cats living in or close to an urban area are at the highest safety risk. The amount of traffic is such that death from road accidents is a major concern. In such environments there are high dog populations, some of which are dangerous. Injury or death from dog attacks is therefore another major source of danger to a feline.

Urban cat populations are also

BE ONE JUMP AHEAD
Seemingly innocuous things, such as doors, can become life-threatening should they suddenly slam shut on a cat due to a strong draught. When windows and external doors are open, be sure internal doors are secured with a doorstop. At all times be one jump ahead of your Bengal in terms of identifying dangerous situations.

Furthermore, their very presence in and around a gentle cat's garden can cause the pet severe stress. This can make it fearful of stepping outside its home. In some instances, it may cause the pet to actually leave its home.

Sadly, if these risks are not enough, there is no shortage of people who will steal a pedigree cat, the more so if it is friendly and outgoing like the Bengal. Add to this the number of abusive people who do not like cats roaming into their gardens, and the scenario is not good. Finally, free-roaming cats also take a heavy toll on local bird and wildlife populations. Bengals are agile tree climbers and excel at bird and squirrel hunting.

Taking these various facts into account, the urban cat is best kept indoors. It can enjoy the benefit of the outdoors if supplied with a roomy aviary-type exercise pen. Some cats can be trained to walk on a lead. This allows outdoor enjoyment, even if only restricted to the garden. When walking your cat in public places, use a harness, which is much safer than a collar.

In contrast to urban situations, the cat living in a rural environment is far safer, the more so if there are no immediate neighbours or busy roads. Even so, it is wise to restrict the cat's outdoor freedom to daylight hours. During the night it is more

THE TRAVELLING CAT

Whenever your cat needs to be taken on a car journey, never let it travel loose in the vehicle, which is illegal. It must always be in its carrying box. If a cat were to go under the clutch or brake pedal when the car was moving, this would be dangerous to all occupants. A cat might also spring from one seat to another, which might distract the driver. This could have disastrous results.

Never leave a cat alone in a car on a hot day. The temperature can rise dramatically to the point that the cat is unable to breathe. It could die of heat stroke. Always leave a window partially open, but not so wide that the agile cat could escape.

extremely high. Far too many cats are living a virtually feral existence. These are tough, street-wise cats that often carry fleas and other parasites that are vectors of disease. Some will be carriers of, or infected with, feline leukaemia and other deadly diseases.

The typical feline family pet can be badly injured if it becomes engaged in fights with these roaming bullies.

likely to be hit by a car or to threaten local wildlife.

Those living between the extremes of isolated areas and busy urban environments should consider the local risk factor. Generally it is best to keep the cat indoors but to provide an outdoor exercise pen.

HOUSEHOLD DANGERS

Within its home, a kitten is best viewed as an accident waiting to happen! The most dangerous room is the kitchen. Hot electric hobs, naked flames from gas rings, boiling pans of food or water, and sinks full of water are obvious hazards. An iron left on its board with cable trailing to the floor is an invitation to a

kitten to jump up—with potentially fatal consequences. Washing machines or spin dryers with clothes in them, and their doors open, are inviting places to nap. Always check the kitty isn't inside if the door has been left open. Cupboards containing poisonous or other dangerous substances should always be kept securely closed.

In the living room, the normal dangers are aquariums without hoods, unguarded fires, electric bar heaters, poisonous indoor plants, trailing electrical wires, and ornaments that may be knocked over by a mischievous kitty. Toilets can be fatal to an over-curious kitten. The same is true of a bath containing water. Keep in mind that most Bengals love to play in water. Balconies should be safeguarded to remove the potential for the kitten to slip and fall.

All cats love warm places to sleep, and clothing out of the spin dryer is a favourite. Keep a close eye on your Bengal whenever you are doing laundry to be sure it doesn't jump in the spin dryer or washing machine.

BOARDING YOUR CAT

Cats do not like to travel and the best alternative is to have a trusted friend, relative or pet-sitter watch your cat in your home. If this is impossible, then you may have to board your cat. You can get recommendations from friends or your veterinary surgeon as to which catteries are reputable. When choosing a boarding house, you should visit the facility beforehand to make certain that it is clean and quiet, and that the personnel are caring and attentive to boarders. You should also enquire about their policies concerning health, vaccinations and neutering.

OTHER DANGERS

Other potential dangers are electric tools left lying about and connected to power outlets—even worse if they are left on, as with bench saws. If the kitten is given freedom to exercise in a garden containing a pond, the kitten must be under constant supervision. Cherished ornaments should be placed out of reach of the kitten, as much for their safety as to any danger they may present to the kitty. It's not always the direct danger of something that can be the problem. If an ornament or similar item crashes to the floor, this can startle the kitten into a panicked departure! The kitten could then fall from a shelf or table in its haste.

Keep your Bengal kitten entertained with cat toys and the like to prevent it from finding amusements of its own.

DANGEROUS DISINFECTANTS

Although owners should disinfect the litter box regularly to prevent disease and illness, some household disinfectants can be harmful to cats. Pine-oil-based cleaners are toxic to cats. DO NOT use them. Products containing Phenol should also be avoided. Bleach is a good disinfectant to use; however, be sure to rinse the litter box thoroughly and air it out to get rid of any fumes.

Feeding Your
BENGAL CAT

Today the feeding of cats has been reduced to its most simple level with the availability of many scientifically prepared commercial diets. However, this fact can result in owners' becoming casual in their approach to the subject. While the main object of a given diet is to provide the ingredients that promote healthy growth and maximum immunity to disease, it also fulfils an important secondary role.

It must maintain in the cat a psychological feeling of well-being that avoids nutritionally related stress problems or syndromes. By ensuring the diet is balanced, of good variety and never monotonous, these dual roles will be achieved. This approach will also avoid the situation of the cat's becoming a finicky eater.

BALANCE AND VARIETY

A balanced diet means one that contains all of the major ingredients—protein, fats, carbohydrates, vitamins and minerals—in the ratios needed to ensure maximum growth and health. Variety means supplying foods in a range of forms that will maintain and stimulate the cat's interest in its meals. Commercially formulated foods come in three levels of moisture: low (dried), semi-moist, and moist (tinned).

Generally, the dried and moist forms are the most popular. Dried cat foods have the advantage they can be left in the cat dish for longer periods of time than can tinned foods. They are ideal for supplying on a free-choice basis. Like the tinned varieties, they come in a range of popular flavours.

In order to meet the specific needs of a kitten, there are specially formulated foods available. These contain higher protein levels needed by a growing kitten. As it grows, the kitten can be slowly weaned onto the adult types. There are also special brands available from vets for any kitten or cat that may have a dietary problem as well as special diets for the older cat. These may need lower ratios of certain ingredients, such as proteins and sodium, so as to reduce the workload of the liver.

Flavours should be rotated so interest in meals is maintained.

DIETARY DIFFERENCES BETWEEN CATS AND DOGS

You should never feed your cat dog food because dogs and cats have different dietary needs. Cats have a much higher need for fats than dogs, and kittens need more than adult cats. Cats also require unusually high levels of dietary protein as compared with those required by dogs. The foods you choose for your cat must supply these essential components.

This also encourages familiarity with different tastes. Naturally, Bengals will display a greater liking for certain flavours and brands than for others.

FRESH FOODS

To add greater variety and interest, there are many fresh foods that Bengals enjoy. Some will be very helpful in cleaning the teeth and exercising jaw muscles. All have the benefit of providing different textures and smells that help stimulate the palate. Feed these foods two or three times a week as treats or occasionally as complete meals.

Cooked poultry, including the skin, but minus the bones, is usually a favourite, as is quality raw or cooked mincemeat. Cooked beef on the bone gives the cat something to enjoy. Cooked white fish, tinned tuna and sardines, are examples of ocean delights. Never feed raw fish; this can prove dangerous, even fatal. Although cats rarely enjoy items such as rice, pasta or cooked vegetables, these can nonetheless be finely chopped and mixed with meats or fish. Some Bengals may develop a taste for them. Various cheeses and scrambled or boiled eggs will often be appreciated—but never give raw eggs.

If the diet is balanced and varied, the addition of vitamin and mineral supplements is unnecessary and can actually prove dangerous. While certain of these compounds are released from the body if in excess, others are not. They are stored and can adversely affect efficient metabolism. If a cat shows loss of condition and disinterest in its food, discuss its diet with a vet.

HOW MUCH TO FEED

Food intake is influenced by many factors. These are the cat's age, activity level, the ambient temperature (more is eaten in the colder months), the cat's breeding state (rearing kittens) and the quality of the food. Always follow the breeder's recommendations on diet until your kitten has settled into your home. Thereafter the needed quantity will increase as the kitten gets older, until full maturity at about two years of age.

As a basic guide, a four-

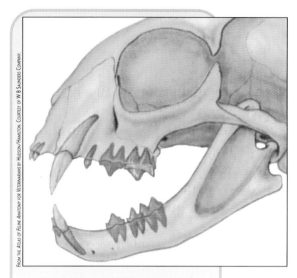

FROM THE ATLAS OF FELINE ANATOMY FOR VETERINARIANS BY HUDSON/HAMILTON. COURTESY OF W B SAUNDERS COMPANY.

MEET THE MEAT-EATERS

Since cats are carnivorous, their teeth are designed to bite and cut. Except for crunching dried foods, cats do very little chewing. They have the fewest teeth of any common domestic mammal—typically 30 (although there are some variations). The canines usually are more developed than the incisors.

EAT YOUR HAIRBALLS AWAY

Food companies have developed formulas containing a wholesome fibre blend that moves ingested hair through the cat's digestive tract, thus minimising the occurrence of hairballs. Tests show that feeding these formulas moved 80% more hair through the digestive tract, meaning fewer hairballs!

month-old kitten will require four meals a day. When the cat reaches six months old, one meal can be dropped. By twelve months of age, only two meals will be required, possibly only one if dried foods are also available on a free-choice basis. As the number of meals is decreased, the quantity must be increased at the meals fed.

FOOD AND WATER CONTAINERS

Bengals are not too fussy over what vessels are used for supplying their food and water, but a few tips are useful. Bengals do not like to eat from dirty dishes anymore than you would. Their food bowls should be

ESTABLISHING DAILY INTAKE

Quoting amounts needed is impossible because of the varying factors mentioned. The best way to establish requirements is on an actual consumption basis. Place a small amount of food on the dish and see how quickly this is eaten. If all is devoured within a few minutes, add a little more. Repeat this until the kitten is satiated and walks away from its dish. Do likewise at the other meals and you will quickly establish daily intake.

MILK AND CATS

Milk, although associated with cats, is not needed once kittenhood has passed. Indeed, excess can create skeletal and other problems. Some cats may become quite ill if given too much. They are unable to digest its lactose content. However, small amounts may be appreciated as a treat. Goat's milk, diluted condensed milk and low-lactose milks are better than cow's milk.

washed after each meal. Water containers should be washed and replenished every day. Purchase large water bowls to give your Bengal some leverage for splashing. Saucers make ideal food plates. Wide feeders from your pet shop are excellent for dried biscuits. Pot or polished metal containers are better buys than plastic. They last longer and are easier to keep clean.

Having a short muzzle, the Bengal does not like to place its head into deep food dishes nor do they like their whiskers to touch the inner walls. Ensure dishes are wide and shallow.

WHERE AND WHEN TO FEED

Usually, the best place to feed a cat is in the kitchen. It is important to place food and water dishes as far away from the litter tray as possible. This could

DRIED FOOD— MORE WATER

If the cat is only given dried foods, it is essential that its water bowl is always full; it will need to drink more. But it is best to give both dried and moist food types. This minimises the risk of urological problems created by pH alkalinity associated with dried diets.

otherwise deter the cat from eating. Cats also like to eat in quiet comfort. Meals should be spread across the entire day. When the number is reduced to two, these should be given in the morning and evening at convenient times. For the Bengal given outdoor freedom, it is best to feed the main meal in the evening. This encourages it to come home at this time. It can then be kept indoors overnight.

IMPORTANT DON'TS

- Do not let your cat become a fussy eater. Cats are not born fussy but are made that way by their owners. Your cat will not starve if given the correct food, but it may try to convince you otherwise. However, a cat that refuses all foods offered may be ill. Contact your vet.
- Do not give a cat sweet and sticky foods. These provide no benefit and, if eaten, will negatively affect normal appetite for wholesome foods.
- Do not feed vitamin and mineral supplements to either kittens or adults unless under advice from a veterinary surgeon. Excess vitamins and minerals can be as bad for your cat's health as a lack of them. They will create potentially dangerous cellular metabolic imbalances.
- Do not give any questionable foods, such as those that smell or look 'off.' If in doubt, discard them. Always store foods in cool, darkened cupboards. Be sure all foods from the freezer and refrigerator are fully thawed.

Bengals, like
all cats, are
meticulous self-
groomers, though
owners must
initiate regular
brushing routines
when their cats
are kittens.

Grooming Your

BENGAL CAT

From the perspective of grooming, the Bengal has an easy non-matting coat. If brushed every day, it will rarely need combing, though this is beneficial. Brisk brushing followed by a polish, using a chamois leather or piece of silk cloth, will maintain the fur in super condition. If you frequently stroke your Bengal, the natural oils on your hand will give the coat a sleek look.

Regular grooming also enables close examination of the cat for any signs of problems. These include fleas or mites, small wounds, abrasions, swellings and bald areas. The grooming process should include inspection of the cat's ears, teeth and nails.

BRUSHING
Place the cat on a table of a height enabling you to comfortably control and groom the kitty. It can be useful to place white paper on the table. If any fleas are present, you will more easily notice them if they are groomed out of the fur. If the grooming is carried out gently, cats enjoy the experience. You should start when your Bengal is still a kitten. Commence by brushing the fur on the back of

Regular brushing will eliminate the amount of hair left on furniture and around your home.

GROOMING EQUIPMENT

For total grooming needs, the following are required:

1. Semi-stiff bristle brush or rubber-pinned brush
2. Fine-toothed comb
3. Flea comb
4. Thin chamois leather and/or a silken cloth
5. Pair of guillotine-type nail trimmers
6. Medium-soft toothbrush
7. Cat toothpaste
8. Supply of cotton wool and cotton buds
9. Bottle of baby oil

favour the tail base or the neck behind the ears. Next, comb with the lie of the fur. Add a final lustre by going over the coat with the chamois.

BATHING

Occasionally, even shorthaired cats may need bathing. This may be of the wet or dry type. For wet baths, using the kitchen sink is preferable to a bath. This saves bending and allows for better control of the cat. To prevent the cat from sliding, use a rubber mat. A spray attachment is more efficient than a jug to wet and rinse the coat. The cat should have its own towels.

The choice of shampoo is important. It should ideally be formulated for cats—do not use one for dogs. This could cause problems on a cat's coat. Baby shampoos are the best alternative. Dry shampoos in powder form are available from pet shops. Alternatives would be talcum

the neck. Work along the back and down the sides, then down the legs and finally the tail. The abdominal area must be brushed more gently as it is very sensitive.

Next, repeat the process using the fine-toothed comb. Then comb against the lie of the hair. This will enable you to see if there are any parasites present. These often

CAT COATS

The long primary hairs of longhaired cats can be almost three times as long as those of a shorthaired cat. The genes for length of hair are independent of the genes for colour. The original colour of cats is the mackerel or tiger-striped pattern. This pattern was inherited from the ancestors of the house cat.

DRY SHAMPOO

A dry bath may be preferred to a wet one during very cold weather or when the cat is not well enough for a water bath. Sprinkle dry shampoo into the coat and give it a good brushing. This will remove excess grease and dirt without being as thorough as a wet bath. Be very sure all the powder is brushed from the fur to avoid potential irritation and consequential scratching.

powder, powdered chalk or heated bran flakes.

The kitten should be bathed by the time it is six months of age. This will familiarise it with the process before it matures. Most Bengals do not mind the bath, provided the owner makes it a pleasant, non-threatening experience.

Grooming should always precede bathing, as this will remove any dead hairs. The key to success lies in ensuring that no water or shampoo is allowed to enter and irritate the eyes or ears. You should be able to cope single-handed with a kitten. However, it may be prudent to have someone else present just in case the adult proves more of a super cat than a kitten!

The water temperature should be warm, never cold or too hot. Prepare a shampoo and water

HAIRBALLS (Trichobezoar)

When cats self-groom, they invariably swallow some of their hairs. Normally these do not create a problem. However, if many dead hairs are in the coat, these may be licked and swallowed to accumulate in the stomach as hairballs. These are more common in longhaired breeds than in those with short hair. Hairballs may create intestinal blockages that may so irritate the cat's intestinal tract that it vomits the hairball or voids it via its faecal matter.

If the hairball is not removed, and the cat displays reduced appetite, veterinary assistance is needed. Regular grooming greatly reduces the risk of this condition. Additionally, a teaspoon of liquid paraffin or other laxative once a week may be helpful in cats prone to this problem. A laxative, however, is unlikely to remove an existing hairball. Pineapple juice containing the enzyme bromelain may break down small furballs. One teaspoonful a day for three days is the recommended dosage.

Use a damp cotton bud or piece of cotton wool to remove wax or debris from your Bengal's ears. Be very careful not to probe inside the ear.

solution before commencing. Have a large towel at hand. Commence by soaking the fur of the neck, then work along the back, sides, legs and tail. Pour shampoo onto the back and work this in all directions until the cat has been fully shampooed. Next, thoroughly rinse all the shampoo away. It is essential that none be left, otherwise it may cause later irritation. Gently but firmly squeeze all water from the coat.

The face can be cleaned using a dampened flannel.

Wrap the kitten in the towel and give it a brisk rubbing until it is as dry as possible. It can then

CLEAN CATS

Cats are self-groomers. They use their barbed tongues and front paws for grooming. Some cats never groom themselves, while others spend up to a third of their waking hours grooming themselves. Licking stimulates certain skin glands that make the coat waterproof.

HAIR, HAIR EVERYWHERE!

Cat's hairs grow denser on the abdomen than on the back. The hairs grow according to both light periodicity (daylight versus dark nights) and temperature. Outdoor cats living in colder climates cast their coats twice a year, in the spring and fall, while house cats do so all year long.

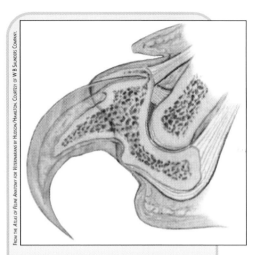

From the Atlas of Feline Anatomy for Veterinarians by Hudson/Hamilton. Courtesy of W B Saunders Company.

be allowed to dry naturally, after which it can be given a final brush and polish. If the cat is normally allowed outdoors, do not allow this for some hours until you are sure the coat is dry. In the colder months it is best to attend to bathing in the early

HAIR GROWTH

Cat's body hairs grow from the follicles, which are connected to the dermis. Tactile hairs (whiskers) are thicker and longer, originating three times deeper than the normal body hairs.

DECLAWING

Declawing is the surgical removal of all of the claw (or nail) and the first toe joint. This practice is heavily frowned upon and even illegal in some countries, such as the United Kingdom. Unfortunately, in some areas of the world this procedure is still performed. Some owners only have the claws from the front feet removed; others do all four feet. An alternative surgical procedure is removing the tendon that allows the cat to protract its claws. This procedure, referred to as a tendonectomy, as compared to an onychectomy (removal of the claws), is less traumatic for the cat. Claws still must be filed and trimmed after a tendonectomy.

Declawing is not always 100% successful. In two-thirds of the cases the cats recovered in 72 hours. Only 4–5% of the cats hadn't recovered within a fortnight. About 3% of the cats had their claws grow back!

The corner of the Bengal's eyes can be gently wiped with damp cotton wool to remove any debris.

evening and keep the cat indoors overnight. The use of a hand dryer is not essential on a short-coated breed, but does shorten the drying time.

EARS, EYES AND NAILS

When inspecting the ears, look for any signs of dirt. This can be gently wiped away using a dampened cotton bud or one with just a little baby or vegetable oil on it. Never attempt to probe into the ear. If the ear is very waxed, this may indicate an health problem. A visit to the vet is recommended. The corner of the eyes can be gently wiped with damp cotton wool to remove any dust that occasionally accumulates.

Inspection of a cat's claws is achieved by firstly restraining the cat while on its back on your lap

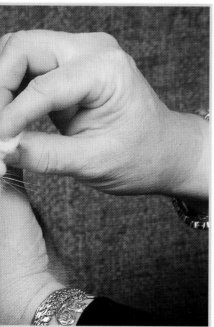

or held against your chest. Hold the paw and apply pressure to the top of this with your thumb. The nail will appear from its sheath. If the nail needs trimming, use the appropriate trimmers.

It is vital that you do not cut into, or even too close to, the quick, which is a blood vessel. This can be seen as a darker area of the nail in pink-clawed cats. It is more difficult, or not possible,

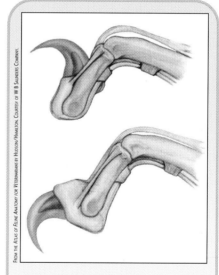

FROM THE ATLAS OF FELINE ANATOMY FOR VETERINARIANS BY HUDSON/HAMILTON, COURTESY OF W B SAUNDERS COMPANY.

(Above) Clipping your Bengal's claws will limit the amount of scratching your cat does in your home. (Below) Tear stains occasionally mar the face of a Bengal. Your local pet shop usually has tear stain remover made for pets.

RETRACTABLE CLAWS

When at rest, a cat's claws are retracted. The muscles hold the claws in their sheaths. The claw is then extended if the cat wishes to attack prey, defend itself, grab an object or climb. That is why your cat's claws are not always visible. This is true for all species of felines except the cheetah, which is unable to retract its claws, except when it is very young.

The eyes of the Bengal should be clear and bright, showing no sign of debris or tearing.

Your vet should check your Bengal's teeth and bite periodically to monitor any decay or abnormalities.

GINGIVITIS (Plasmocytic-Lymphocytic Stomatitis)

There are many causes of this condition. But the end result is the same—bad breath, excessive plaque, tooth loss and, almost certainly, pain. The cat salivates excessively, starts to eat less and consequently loses weight. On inspection, the gums are swollen, especially in the area of the premolar and molar teeth. They bleed easily. There are various treatments, such as antibiotics, immunostimulants and disinfectant mouth gels. However, these invariably prove short-term and merely delay the inevitable treatment of extraction.

Prevention avoids this painful condition. Regular tooth inspection and cleaning, plus provision of hard-food items, such as cat biscuits, achieve this to a large extent. There are also special cat chews made of dried fish that help clean the teeth. They also contain antibacterial enzymes that minimise or prevent secondary bacteria from accumu-lating. Ask for these at your pet shop or vet's surgery. Gingivitis may commence in kittens, so do not think it is something that only occurs in older cats.

to see the quick in dark-coloured nails. In such instances, trim less. You may need a helper to do the trimming or the holding. If in doubt, let your vet do this for you. If cats have ample access to scratching posts, they will only infrequently, if ever, require their nails to be trimmed.

TEETH

From its youngest days, your kitten should become familiar with having its teeth cleaned. Many owners do not give these the attention they should. This has become progressively more important due to the soft diet regimens of modern cats. Initially, gently rub the kitten's teeth using a soft cloth on which cat toothpaste has been placed. This will accustom the kitten to having its teeth touched as well as to the taste of the tooth cleaner. When this is no problem for the kitten, you can progress to a soft toothbrush and ultimately one of medium hardness. Periodically let your vet check the cat's mouth.

SETTING THE GROUND RULES

From the outset you must determine the ground rules and stick to them. Always remember that your companion's patterns of behaviour begin to form from the moment it first arrives at your home. If the future adult is not to be given outdoor freedom, then do not let it outdoors as a kitten. If any rooms are to be out of bounds to the adult, then do not let the kitten into them. Stability is vital in a cat's life; without it, the result will be stress and its related behavioural changes.

Ground rules of how to handle the kitten and to respect its privacy when sleeping should be instilled into all children. The cat's meals should be given at about the same time each day. This will have the secondary advantage that the pet's toilet habits will be more predictable.

By and large, Bengals are remarkably easy to live with. They are fastidious in their personal habits related to grooming and toilet routines and basically require very little of their owners. Nonetheless, behavioural problems in cats can occur, and an owner should understand all the possible causes and solutions. You may never encounter a single problem with your Bengal, but it pays to be prepared should your feline charge disrupt your domestic bliss.

THE BASIS OF TRAINING

The most effective means of training a cat is via reinforcement of success. A cat learning from lavish praise of doing what is required will want to repeat the action to gain more affection. There are no potential negative side effects. Conversely, when scolding or other methods of discipline are used, there is always the possibility the cat will not relate the punishment to what the owner had intended.

For example, you cannot discipline for something done in the past. The past is anything much longer than a few minutes ago. If you call the cat to you to punish it for something done hours earlier, it cannot comprehend that action. It will relate the discipline to the act of going to you when called! This will create insecurity in the pet, increasing the risk that more problems will develop.

REMEDIAL METHODS

When faced with a problem, firstly try to pinpoint the likely cause(s). Next, consider the remedial options. Be sure these will not result in negative side effects linked to you. Always be the paragon of patience. Some problems may be extremely complex and deeply rooted within the cat's behaviour patterns. As such, they are habits not easily changed, and often difficult to analyse. In discussing the following problems, it is hoped you will understand the basic ways in which to correct other unwanted patterns of behaviour that might occur. But always remember it is far better to avoid a problem than correct it.

THE LITTER TRAY

A very common problem for some owners is that their cat starts to attend to its toiletry needs anywhere other than in its litter tray. The problem may become apparent from the time the kitten gets to its new home, or it may develop at any time during its life.

CATS AND OTHER PETS

If you already have a pet cat or cats, or dogs, or almost any other animal that isn't small, creeping or crawling, your cat can usually be socialised so the other pet and the cat will tolerate each other. In many cases, cats and dogs become quite friendly and attached to each other, often making frequent physical contacts, sleeping together or even sharing each other's food.

So, let us start from the beginning and try to avoid the situation.

Until you are satisfied that the kitten is using its litter tray, do not give it access to carpeted rooms. The youngster should already have been litter trained well before you obtained it. You should obtain a litter tray similar to the one it is already familiar with. It is also important that the same brand of litter is used, at least initially. Place the tray in a quiet spot so the kitten has privacy when attending to its needs.

CAUSES OF LITTER-BOX PROBLEMS

1. The litter tray is dirty. Cats never like to use a previously fouled tray.
2. The litter has been changed to one of a different texture that the cat does not like. Generally the finer-grained litters are the most favoured.
3. A scented litter is being used to mask odours. The cat may not like the scent. Such litters should not be necessary if the tray is regularly cleaned.
4. The tray is regularly cleaned, but an ammonium or pine-based disinfectant is being used. This may aggravate the cat's sensitive nasal mucous membranes. Additionally, the phenols in pine are dangerous to cats.
5. The litter tray is located too close to the cat's food and water bowls. Cats do not like to eat near litter trays or to defecate/urinate close to their feeding areas.
6. Another cat or free-roaming pet has been added to the household and is causing the cat stress. In multi-cat households, two or more trays may be needed.
7. There is insufficient litter in the tray. There should be about 2 inches of litter depth.
8. The cat has developed a fear of using the tray due to an upsetting experience. For instance, the owner may have caught the cat as it finished using the tray in order that it could be given a medicine. Children may be disturbing it while it is relieving itself.
9. The cat is ill (or elderly) and is unable to control its bowel movements. Veterinary attention is required.
10. The cat, because of one or more of the previous problems, has established other more favourable areas.

A kitten will need to relieve itself shortly after it has eaten, exercised, or slept. Watch it carefully at these times. If it stoops to attend to its needs other than in the litter tray, calmly lift it into its tray and scratch at the litter. Never shout or panic the kitty by making a sudden rush for it. If it does what is hoped, give it lots of praise. If it steps out of the tray without relieving itself, gently place it back in for a few seconds.

If nothing happens, be patient and wait, then repeat the process. If it fouls the kitchen floor when you are not watching, simply clean this up and wait for the next opportunity to transport the kitten to its tray. It rarely takes long for a kitten to consistently use this. Be very sure the tray is kept spotless. Cats do not like to use a fouled tray. Every few days, give the cat tray a good wash using soapy water and always rinse it thoroughly. Allow it to dry, then fill the tray with litter to depth of about 4–5 cms (1.5–2 inches).

By identifying the cause(s) of litter-box problems, the correction is often self-evident. However, once the cause has been corrected, this is only part of the solution.

Next, the habit of fouling other places must be overcome. Where possible, do not let the cat enter rooms it has started to foul until the odour has had time to fully disperse. Wash the area of the accident, then treat carpets and soft furnishings with an odour neutraliser (not an air freshener) from your pet shop or vet.

If the cat cannot be prevented from entering certain rooms, then cover previously fouled areas with plastic sheeting or tinfoil. Also, place a litter tray in the fouled room while the retraining is underway. It may help if a different size, type or colour of tray is used. Always remember

MARKING TERRITORY

Cats are geographical by nature and they mark their territories in the usual way...by spraying their urine. The frequency of spraying is amazing! A non-breeding male cat that is not within its own turf will spray about 13 times an hour while travelling through the new territory. A breeding male will spray almost twice as much. One reports states that free-ranging males spray 62.6 times an hour—that's more than once a minute!

Cat urine is recognisable for at least 24 hours and male cats spend a lot of time sniffing the area. Females spend less time, but both sexes easily recognise the urine from male cats that are strange to the area.

TIDY TOILETING

During the kitten's stay in the nest box, the mother will assist or even stimulate bowel and urine elimination, at least for the first month of the kitten's life. The mother also does the clean-up work in the nest box. But once the kitten is older, it becomes capable of relieving itself out of the nest box. Usually the kitten likes sand, soft earth or something that seems absorbent and is easily moved with its paws. By the time the kitten is two months old, it should develop the discipline of covering its elimination. Not all kittens develop this discipline, though the use of an absorbent clay litter seems to be helpful in developing this discipline in young cats. Your local pet shop will have various cat litters to offer you.

MAN MEETS CAT

Early man, perhaps 8000 years ago, started his symbiotic relationship with domestic cats, *Felis catus* or *Felis domesticus*. The cats killed and ate the rats and mice and probably anything else which crawled and was small, which early man attracted and considered as pests. Early man reciprocated by allowing the cat to sleep in his cave, hut or tent. Cats, being essentially nocturnal, kept the small mammals (rats, mice, etc.) from disturbing the sleep of early man.

As early man evolved to modern man, the domestic cat came along as an aid to pest control. This was especially true of peoples who farmed, as farmers were plagued with rodents. Though most cats were not selectively bred for their predatory skills, it was obvious that those cats that were the best hunters were more successful in evolutionary terms than the cats that were more meek. Modern cats have changed very little from the cats from which they descended. There are still, today, cats that are very predatory, attacking small mammals and birds; there are also meek cats which, unless fed by their owners, would perish in a competitive cat society.

It has been shown repeatedly that if kittens are socialised in a proper manner, they will become peaceful pets. This includes lions and tigers. If the kittens are not socialised properly, they revert immediately to their aggressive, predatory behaviours.

THE TRUTH ABOUT CATS AND DOGS

Cats are unique in having the scrotum fully haired, a marked difference from their canine counterparts. This led one early observer to say that cats were not small dogs! Dogs were domesticated well before cats since cats only served to protect the abode of the owner from rodents, while dogs served as guards, hunters, herders, exterminators and as loyal companions that were readily trainable. Cats have always been more independent and less trainable.

that the older cat may have problems with bowel control. An extra litter tray at another location in the home will usually remedy this situation.

SCENT MARKING

Both sexes scent mark, though males are more prolific. It is a means of advertising their presence in a territory, thus an integral part of their natural behaviour. Spraying is usually done against a vertical surface. It tells other males that the individual is residing in that territory. More to the point, it will tell a female that a male lives close by—or, with females, it will tell the male that a female is in the area. It is thus a very important part of a cat's social language.

Neutered cats have little need to mark their territory or leave their 'calling' card to attract mates. They are far less likely to spray than those which are not altered. However, scent marking may commence when the cat is attempting to assert its position in the household.

To overcome the problem of scent marking, the first need is to identify if there is an obvious specific cause. In multi-cat households, it also requires positive identification of the sprayer(s) and the favoured spraying surface. Giving the cat more freedom and its own sleeping place, if it does not have one, may be helpful. Covering the sprayed surface with plastic sheeting, or a cloth impregnated with a scent the cat does not like (such as lemon, vinegar or bleach) may be successful. Spraying the cat with a water pistol when catching it in the action is a common ploy. Veterinary treatment with the hormone progesterone may prove effective—discuss this with your vet.

SCRATCHING

Scratching is a normal feline characteristic. Unfortunately, house cats tend to destroy the furniture to satisfy their need to scratch. Feral or outdoor cats usually attack a tree because trees are readily accessible and the bark

Provide your Bengals with suitable places to scratch and exercise their claws. Scratching is a normal activity for all cats, and owners must make wise choices to deter their Bengals from using the furniture and carpets for this purpose.

of the tree suits their needs perfectly. If the outdoor cat lives in a pride, it will scratch more than a solitary feral cat. The reasons for this are known. When cats scratch, they leave telltale marks. Parts of the nail's sheath exudate from glands located between their claws, and the visual aspects are the marks which cats leave to impress or advertise their presence.

Owners of cats that scratch should not consider the scratching as an aggressive behavioural

CAUSES OF SCENT MARKING

1. Another cat, or pet, has been introduced to the household. It may be bullying the resident cat. This problem may resolve itself when the two get to know each other. The more cats there are, the longer it may take for the situation to be resolved. Much will depend on the space within which the cats may roam and whether they are able to avoid those they dislike.

2. The birth of a new family member may annoy the cat for a while, especially if its owner suddenly gives it less attention.

3. A friend staying in the home for a few days may not like cats. If 'shooed' away a number of times, the cat may feel it should assert its position and mark it.

4. If the cat is given outdoor freedom, a bully may have moved into the territory. Having lost control of its own garden, the pet may assert its territorial boundaries within its home. If a cat flap is used, another cat may be entering the home and this will trigger the resident to scent mark.

disorder. It is normal for cats to scratch. Keeping your cat's claws clipped or filed so they are as short as possible without causing bleeding may inhibit scratching. Your vet can teach you how to do this. Clipping and filing should be

started when the kitten is very young. Starting this when the cat has matured is much more difficult and may even be dangerous.

There are ways to control annoying cat scratching. Certainly,

Bengals are among the most natural of all cats, retaining most of the instincts of their not-so-distant wild ancestors. If you can properly supervise your Bengal outdoors, allow it to spend an hour or so outside to exercise and hear the call of the wild.

CAT SCRATCH DISEASE

An objectionable habit of many poorly raised kittens is their exuberant jumping to greet you. This flying jump may result in the kitten's being attached to your body; otherwise it will fall to the floor and may injure itself. In the attachment process, your skin will usually be pierced, and this is a health concern. All cat scratches and bites should be thoroughly cleaned with an antiseptic soap. If a sore appears at the site of the wound, you should visit your family doctor immediately.

Cat scratch disease is a well-known problem. It is caused by a bacterium *(Rochalimaea henselae)* that is usually easily treated with antibiotics. However, more and more cases show resistance to the usual antibiotics.

Untreated cat scratch fever may result in an enlargement of the lymph nodes, imitating a cancerous condition known as lymphoma. Interestingly enough, the lymph nodes, upon biopsy, may show large Reid-Sternberg cells, which are a characteristic of Hodgkins lymphoma. The bottom line is that cat scratches should be taken seriously.

SCRATCHING FURNITURE

All cats need to scratch in order to maintain their claws in good condition. For this reason, one or more scratching posts strategically placed in the cat's most-used rooms will normally prevent the problem. Place the post in front of the scratched furniture. It can be moved steadily further away once the furniture is ignored. This is a problem that may become more manifest when cats that are not allowed outdoors have insufficient indoor provisions to scratch.

the easiest way is to present your cat with an acceptable cat scratching post. These are usually available at most local pet shops. The post should be covered with a material that is to your cat's liking. If your cat has already indicated what it likes to scratch, it usually is a good idea to cover the post with this same material. Veterinary surgeons often suggest that you use sandpaper, as this will reduce the cat's nails quickly and it will not have the urge to scratch. Certainly using hemp, carpeting, cotton towelling or bark is worth a try. Once the cat uses the post, it usually will have neither a desire nor a need to scratch any place else.

Besides the physical need to scratch, many cats have a psychological need to scratch. This is evidenced by where they scratch versus what they scratch. Often cats prefer semi-darkness. Some prefer flat surfaces and not vertical surfaces. Some prefer public areas in which their human friends are present instead of secretive areas. It may be stress-related, as with scent marking, because scratching is another territorial-marker behaviour. In any case, the idea is to get your cat to scratch the post and not the carpets, furniture, drapes or duvet on your bed.

Introduce your cat to the post by rubbing its paws on the post, hoping it will take the hint.

Oftentimes the cat voluntarily attacks the post. Unfortunately, oftentimes it doesn't. If you catch your cat scratching in a forbidden area, startle it with a loud shout, banging a folded newspaper against your hand, or something else that will take its attention away from scratching. *Never* hit the cat. This will only get a defensive reaction that might be problematic.

RUBBISH RUMMAGING

Cats are inquisitive and may decide to have a good look through any interesting rubbish bins that are exuding an enticing odour. Normally, the answer is to remove the bin. However, if the attraction always seems to be kitchen rubbish, there may be a nutritional problem. The cat may be searching for food because it is being underfed! It may alternatively be receiving an unbalanced diet and is trying to satisfy its inner need for a given missing ingredient.

Another possibility, and one which may be more appropriate to the indoors-only cat, is boredom or loneliness. These conditions can only be remedied by greater interaction between owner and cat and/or obtaining a companion feline.

Clearly the cause should be identified. The immediate solution is to place the rubbish bin in a cupboard or similar place that is out of the cat's reach. This type of solution is called removal of the re-enforcer. It is a common method of overcoming problems across a number of unwanted behaviours. However, it does not correct the underlying problem that must still be addressed.

The first-time cat owner should not think that the problems discussed will likely be encountered. They are only met when the cat's environment is lacking in some way. Finally, if a problem is found and you are not able to remedy it, do seek the advice of your vet or breeder.

If your Bengal is presenting problems to you, contact your breeder for some certain insight and solutions.

Breeding Your
BENGAL CAT

While the idea of becoming a breeder may appeal to many owners, the reality is more difficult than is often appreciated. It requires dedication, considerable investment of time and money, and the ability to cope with many heart-wrenching decisions and failures.

It would be quite impossible to discuss the complexities of practical breeding in only one chapter, so we will consider the important requirements of being a breeder plus some basic feline reproductive information. This will enable you to better determine if, indeed, this aspect of the hobby is for you.

BEING A BREEDER
Apart from great affection for the breed, a successful breeding programme requires quantifiable objectives. Foremost among these is the rearing of healthy kittens free from known diseases. Next is the desire to produce offspring that are as good as, indeed better than, their parents.

Such objectives ensure that a breeder will endeavour to maintain standards and reduce or

TOO MANY CATS
There are already too many cats in the world. In many countries, thousands of pathetic-looking felines can be seen wandering the streets in a badly emaciated state. They live tormented lives and have become a major social problem in many areas. There can be no excuse for these feral populations in developed Western nations. Quite frankly, some people who own cats, including some pedigreed owners, lack a sense of responsibility.

Cats allowed to roam in a non-neutered state are by far the main reason for the overpopulation problem. Unless a cat is of show or breeding quality, there is not a single justification for it to be bred or to remain in a non-neutered state. If your cat was purchased as a pet, you should help to resolve this global problem by having it neutered at the earliest possible date. This will make it a far healthier, happier and less problematic pet.

remove from the cat population any instances of dangerous diseases and conditions. Only stock registered and tested free of major diseases should ever be used. Adopting such a policy helps to counteract those who breed from inferior and often unhealthy cats.

To be a successful breeder, you will need to become involved in the competition side of the hobby. Only via this route will you be able to determine whether your programme is successful or not. Always remember that even the top-winning breeders still produce quite a high percentage of kittens that will only be of pet quality. There will be many disappointments along the road to even modest success.

THE DISADVANTAGES OF BREEDING

There are many rewards to be gained from breeding but the disadvantages should also be carefully considered. Kittens are demanding, especially once they are over three weeks of age. Rearing, vaccination, registration and veterinary bills will be costly. Any thoughts of profit should be dispelled. Homes must be found for the kittens, which will entail receiving many telephone calls—some at very inconvenient hours.

Many potential buyers will prove to be either unsuitable or 'time wasters' looking for the

TOM FOOLERY

A non-neutered male cat kept as a single pet has little or no value for breeding purposes. It must be exhibited so it can gain some fame. The owner must have modern facilities to house both males and females. Females are always serviced at the home of the stud owner. This is extra responsibility and cost.

Such a male cannot be given any freedom to roam. If the tom is kept indoors, its scent-marking odours will often become intolerable. Even kept outdoors in a suitable cat pen, it will spray regularly to attract the attention of any females in the area. Toms are more assertive and often more aggressive than neutered males.

If they are allowed any outdoor freedom, they will become involved in battles with the local toms. Consequently, they will soon lose their handsome looks! Most cat breeders do not even keep males because of the problems and costs they entail. These cats are best kept in catteries where the owners have the time, the funds and everything else needed to justify their retention.

cheapest pedigreed cat obtainable. Kittens may die, while cats of any age could test positive for a major disease. They may have to be put to sleep or given to a caring person who understands the problem.

CAVEAT EMPTOR

When purchasing a kitten for breeding, make certain that the seller knows what your intentions are. If a kitten is registered on the non-active register, this means it was not considered by its breeder to be good enough for breeding. Any kittens bred from such a cat cannot be registered. You should also check that the mother of the kitten/young adult you are interested in has tested negative for feline leukaemia and that all other vaccinations are current.

WHAT'S A PEDIGREE WORTH?

When choosing breeding stock, never be dazzled by a pedigree. No matter how illustrious this is, it is only ever as good as the cat that bears it. If the cat is mediocre, then its prestigious pedigree is worthless from a breeding perspective. There are many other pitfalls for the novice when judging the value of a breeding line. These you must research in larger, more specialised books.

Owning a number of cats will mean investing in cat pens. When females come into heat, they will try to escape and mate with any local tom with a twinkle in his eye! Their scent and calls will attract roving Romeos who will gather near your home and involve themselves in a series of raucous battles. Holidays and matings will need to be planned around hoped-for litter dates. All in all, owning even one or two breeding females is a major commitment.

Before deciding whether breeding really is something you want to do, you should consider neutering your Bengal and becoming an exhibitor. When you have exhibited a number of times, your knowledge of cats will be greater, as will your contacts. You will be more aware of what quality is all about and what it will cost for a well-bred female. Consider this an apprenticeship. Whether you then become a breeder, remain an exhibitor, or prefer life as a pet owner, you will be glad you heeded the words of advice given here.

STOCK SELECTION

Stock selection revolves around health, quality, sex and age. Before these are discussed, it should be stated that many beginners unwisely rush this process. It is essential that ample time be devoted to researching the source of your Bengal stock. This decision will influence a novice breeder's entire future endeavours.

HEALTH

Cats should only be obtained from a breeder whose stock has been tested negative for FeLV, FIP and FIV. The stock should be current on all vaccinations and worm treatments. Additionally, its blood type should be known so as to avoid incompatibility problems.

QUALITY

This must come in two forms. One is in the individual cat's appearance; the other is in its genetic ability to pass on the quality of its parents. The best way of obtaining these paired needs is to obtain initial stock from a breeder having a proven record of success with Bengals.

THE MALE STUD

The selection of a suitable stud should have been planned months before, as it can take some time to find the best male to use. It is preferred that the breeding lines of the stud are compatible with those of the female, meaning both pedigrees will carry a number of the same individuals in them. This is termed line-breeding. The ideal male will excel in those features that are considered weak in the female. You may read in other books that if a female is weak in a given feature, the ideal stud will be the total opposite. However, this can be misleading.

If the female has an overly long tail, what you do not need is a stud with a short tail. Rather, his tail should be as near the ideal length as possible. Genetically, this will improve tail length in your line without introducing unwanted genetic variance in your stock. Compensatory matings, such as short tail to long tail, will create such a variance. Once a male has been selected, ensure all his papers and vaccinations are in order. The female will be taken to the stud and left with him for a few days.

THE BREEDING QUEEN

A female used for breeding purposes is called a queen. The principal requirement of such a cat is that she is an excellent example of the breed. This does not mean she must be a show winner. Many a winning exhibition cat has proved to have little breeding value. This is because a show cat gains success purely on its appearance; however, it may not pass those looks to its offspring.

A good breeding female may lack that extra something needed to be a top winner. Yet, she may pass on most of her excellent features to her offspring. Much will depend on the breeding line from which she was produced. Therefore any potential breeder must research existing breeders to ascertain which have good track records of producing consistently high-quality cats. In truth, and sadly, few newcomers in their haste to become breeders make this extra effort. This can result in becoming disillusioned if the female produces only average to inferior kittens.

Being well acquainted with the breed's standard will be advantageous when seeking foundation stock. A female show cat attains her titles based on her appearance, but she may not pass on those looks to her offspring. Another cat that is very sound may pass on most of her good points and thus be more valuable for breeding. Of course, all litters will be influenced by the quality of the tom used. He will account for 50% of the offspring's genes. When viewing a litter of kittens, never forget that they are the result of the genes of two cats.

Sex

The beginner should only obtain females. The best advice is to commence with just one very sound female. By the time you have exhibited her and gained more knowledge about the finer points of the breed, you will be far better informed to decide what true quality is all about. By then, you will also have made many contacts on the show circuit. Alternatively, you may decide breeding is not for you and will have invested only a minimum of time and money. A male is not needed until a breeder has become established. Even then, owning one is not essential to success. There is no shortage of quality studs. Males create many problems that the novice can do without. Once you have gained experience, you can decide if owning a male would be of any particular benefit.

AGE

There is no specific age at which stock should be purchased, but the following are suggested:

1. Most people purchase young kittens so they can enjoy them. However, with such youngsters, their ultimate quality is harder to assess.
2. Chances are improved if a kitten has already won awards in shows. This will be when she is 14 weeks to 9 months of age, but she will be more costly.
3. A quality young female that has already produced offspring is a prudent choice but will be the most expensive option and most difficult to find.

THE BREEDING PROCESS

Sexual maturity in cats may come as early as four months of age. Breeding should not be considered until the female is at least

CAT CALLS

Females left in a non-spayed state are far more at risk from diseases and infections of the uterus. When in heat, the female becomes unusually affectionate and provocative. Her calls, a sound once heard never forgotten, can become extremely annoying if she is left unmated.

ROAMING ROMEOS

Males cats, toms, have extended testicles very early in life. By about nine months of age, the tom is capable of mating with a queen. Both queens and toms are polygamous and it is not uncommon for a queen to have a litter containing kittens fathered by different toms.

twelve months old, especially in the slow-maturing breeds such as those of Persian and European stock ancestry. A young cat barely out of her kitten stage may not have the required physical or psychological stability to produce and raise a vigorous litter. After

The litter size will generally be two to five. Kittens are born blind and helpless, but develop rapidly. Their eyes open about the seventh day. By 21 days they start exploring. At this time they will also be sampling solid foods. By eight weeks they can be vaccinated and neutered if required. Weaning normally

THE HEAT IS ON

Most female cats reach sexual maturity by the time they are 28 weeks old. Females normally accept males from late winter to early fall, about a six-month period. They have a reproductive cycle of about two weeks and are in heat for about one of the two weeks. Intercourse causes the female to ovulate and pregnancy may last for about 64 days, perhaps longer in cold climates and shorter in the tropics.

her first heat, a female will normally come into heat again every two to three weeks and continue to do so until mated. The actual oestrous period lasts three to eight days. It is during this time that she is receptive to a male.

Once the mating has been successful, the time between fertilisation and birth of the young, known as the gestation period, is in the range 59 to 67 days, 63 or 64 days being typical.

commences by the age of six weeks and is completed within two to three weeks. Kittens can go to a new home when 12 weeks old, though 14 to 16 weeks of age is preferred.

During this period you must decide if you wish to register the kittens or merely 'declare' them. This allows them to be registered at a later time. Obtain the necessary information and forms from your cat registration authority. You should also consider the benefits of registering your own breeder prefix. This, however, is only worthwhile if you intend to breed on a more-than-casual basis. If you have decided that certain kittens are unsuitable for showing/breeding, do consider early neutering.

NEWBORN KITTENS

Most kittens are born with body hair. Their ears and eyes, however, remain closed for about two weeks, though some ears and eyes become functional after 72 hours. Kittens should be allowed to nurse for seven weeks, longer if they will not readily eat and drink from a plate. If allowed to nurse, most kittens will stay on their mother's milk for two months or more.

Kittens should start weaning when they are six weeks old; they should be completely weaned by the time they are nine weeks old.

Exhibiting Your
BENGAL CAT

Without shows, the cat fancy could not exist. There would be only a handful of breeds as compared with today's ever-growing list. There would be fewer colour patterns and far less public awareness of cats. Given the great importance of shows to the cat fancy, it is perhaps a little surprising, and disappointing, that the majority of cat owners have never visited a feline exhibition.

Shows such as the National and the Supreme of Britain, or their equivalents in other countries, are the shop windows of the world of domestic cats. They are meeting places where breeders from all over the country compete to determine how well their breeding programmes are developing. A show is also a major social event on the cat calendar.

Whether a potential pet owner or breeder of the future, you should visit one or two shows. It is a great day out for the whole family. Apart from the wonderful selection of breeds, there are also many trade stands. If a cat product is available, it will be seen at the large exhibitions.

Many of the national clubs

CLASSES AT SHOWS

Open	Any cat of the specified breed.
Novice	Cats that have never won a first prize.
Limit	Cats that have not won more than first prizes.
Junior	Cats over nine months of age but less than two years on the day of the show.
Senior	Cats over two years old.
Visitors	Cats living a given distance away from the show venue.
Assessment	Experimental breeds, which have an approved standard.
Aristocrat	Cats with one or two Challenge Certificates (or Premiers for neuters) so are not yet full Champions/Premiers.

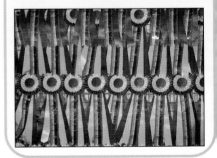

and magazines have stands. The two major shows mentioned are held in the winter months, usually November and December. However, there are hundreds of other shows staged during the year in various parts of the country. They range from small local club events to major championship breed shows and are usually advertised in the cat magazines. Your ruling cat association can also supply a list of shows.

SHOW ORGANISATION

So you will have some idea of how things are organised, the following information will be helpful. You will learn even more by purchasing the show catalogue. This contains the names and addresses of the exhibitors and details of their cats. It also lists the prizes, indicates the show regulations and carries many interesting advertisements.

A major show revolves around three broad categories of cats:
1. Unaltered cats, meaning those that are capable of breeding.
2. Neuters.
3. Non-pedigree cats.

There is, thus, the opportunity for every type of cat, from the best of Bengals to the everyday 'moggie' pets, to take part. These three broad categories are divided into various sections. For example, the unaltered and neuters are divided into their

'VETTING IN'

In England, cats are examined by a veterinary surgeon upon arrival to a show to make sure that they appear healthy. This process is called 'vetting in.' If the cat is rejected, it can not be exhibited again until it receives a 'clearance certificate.' The reasons for rejection are stated in the rule book, which can be obtained at the show.

respective sections, such as Longhair, Semi-Longhair, British, Foreign, Siamese and so on.

There are many more classes other than those mentioned. These include club classes and those for kittens and non-pedigree cats.

JUDGING

There are two ways cats can be judged. One is pen judging, the other is bench or ring judging. In Britain, pen judging is the normal method, though bench judging is used for Best in Show. In pen judging, the judge moves around the cat pens. The cat gaining the most points when compared to the standard wins. In bench judging, stewards take the cats to the judge.

If a cat wins its class, it then competes against other class winners. By this process of elimination, a cat may go on to win Best of Breed award. It then competes against other breed winners for Best in Group award. The group winners compete for the Best in Show award.

A breeder can gather a number of awards during the course of a show. Even those who do not own the very best cats can take pride in gaining second, third, fourth and recommended, especially if won at the larger shows. By progression, the top cat at a show will win its class, its breed, its section, and ultimately become the Best in Show Exhibit. The titles a cat can win commence with that of Champion, or Premier in the case of neuters. A Grand Champion is made after winning in competition with others of its same status. The same applies to a Grand Premier. The judging system may vary from one country to another but the basis remains as outlined.

THE SHOW CAT

When a cat is seen preening in its pen, the hard work that has gone into its preparation is rarely appreciated. Exhibits must be in peak condition and their coats in full bloom. The potential exhibit must be gradually trained to spend hours within its show pen. It must display no fear or aggression towards strangers, such as the stewards or the judges. These must be able to physically examine it, including its ears and teeth; it also involves being lifted into the air. If a cat scratches or bites a judge, or any other show official, it is automatically withdrawn from the show. A repeat of this in the future would

ON THE CONTINENT AND BEYOND...

In Britain, the title of UK Grand Champion or Premier is won in competition with other Grand titleholders. In mainland Europe, cats can become International Champions. More British cats are expected to become International Champions with the recent introduction of passports for cats, allowing cats to compete more freely on the Continent and beyond. In countries other than Britain, the way in which shows are organised and titles achieved do differ somewhat. However, they broadly follow the outline discussed here.

result, in most instances, in the cat's show career being terminated by the ruling association.

Apart from being comfortable with people peering into its pen, the cat must be able to endure long journeys to the show venue. Unless trained, the cat may become a nervous, aggressive feline that will have a very short show career.

Obviously, the cat must display quality. This means having none of the major faults that would prevent it from gaining a first prize. These are listed in the breed standard. The meaning of quality is very flexible. You do not need to own a potential champion to be a successful exhibitor. The cat must also be registered with the association under whose rules the show is being run. In Britain this will be the GCCF or The Cat Association of Britain.

As in anything competitive, exhibits can gain prizes at the lower levels of a hobby without having any realistic chance of awards in the major shows. Owning such exhibits is often part of a top breeder/exhibitor's portfolio from their early days in the hobby. Others may never move beyond the smaller shows but still gain reputations for owing sound stock. They thoroughly enjoy being involved at their given level.

If the idea of exhibiting

BECOMING AN EXHIBITOR

Before any hobbyist enters a show, he is advised to join a local cat club. Here, hobbyists will meet local breeders who will not only assess their cats for them but also provide help on many other topics. The novice exhibitor could attend one or two shows with an exhibitor in order to learn the ropes. During this period, he can become familiar with the show rules and regulations. These are quite extensive, intended to safeguard the best interests of the hobby, the exhibitors and, most importantly, the cats.

It is of interest to note that some breeders own cats in partnership with other fanciers. This is useful when one person enjoys the breeding side and the other the exhibition side. It enables both to really be involved in the hobby to a level that might not have been possible for either on his own. So, whether you fancy being an exhibitor or you just love cats, do make a point of visiting the next major show in your area.

appeals to you, the best way to make a start is to join a local club. There you not only will be advised on all procedures but will assuredly make many new cat-loving friends. Exhibiting can be costly in cash and time, but you can focus on the more local shows while attending the larger ones as a visitor.

Maintaining a cat in the peak of good health revolves around the implementation of a sound husbandry strategy. At the basic level, this means being responsible about feeding, cleanliness, and grooming. However, in spite of an owner's best efforts in these matters, cats may still become ill due to other causes. Although owners can attempt to prevent, identify and react to problems, only a vet is qualified to diagnose and suggest and/or effect remedies. Attempts by owners or 'informed' friends to diagnose and treat for specific diseases are dangerous and potentially life-threatening to the cat.

SELECTING A VETERINARY SURGEON

Your selection of a veterinary surgeon should not be based upon personality (as most are) but upon convenience to your home. You want a vet who is close because you might have emergencies or need to make multiple visits for treatments. You want a vet who has services that you might require such as nail clipping and bathing, as well as sophisticated pet supplies and a good reputation for ability and responsiveness. There is nothing more frustrating than having to wait a day or more to get a response from your veterinary surgeon.

All veterinary surgeons are licensed and their diplomas and/or certificates should be displayed in their waiting rooms. There are, however, many veterinary specialities that usually require further studies and internships. There are specialists in heart problems (veterinary cardiologists), skin problems (veterinary dermatologists), teeth and gum problems (veterinary dentists), eye problems (veterinary ophthalmologists) and x-rays (veterinary radiologists), as well as vets who have specialities in reproduction, nutrition and behaviour. Most veterinary surgeons do routine surgery, such as neutering and stitching up wounds. When the problem affecting your cat is serious, it is not unusual or impudent to get another medical opinion, although in Britain you are obliged to advise the vets concerned about this. You might also want to compare costs among several veterinary surgeons. Sophisticated health care and veterinary services can be very costly. It is not infrequent that important decisions are based upon financial considerations.

PREVENTATIVE MEDICINE

It is much easier, less costly and more effective to practise preventative medicine than to fight bouts of illness and disease. Properly bred kittens come from parents who were selected based upon their genetic disease profile. Their mothers should have been vaccinated, free of all internal and external parasites and properly nourished. For these reasons, a visit to the veterinary surgeon who cared for the queen is recommended. The queen can pass on disease resistance to her kittens, which can last for eight to ten weeks. She can also pass on parasites and many infections. That's why you should visit the veterinary surgeon who cared for the queen.

VACCINATIONS

Most vaccinations are given by injection and should only be done by a veterinary surgeon. Both he

Your Bengal should visit the veterinary surgeon annually for its check-up, vaccinations and general advice. This is Topspot Kashmir, owned by Jaime Gardner.

A LONG, HEALTHY LIFE

As veterinary surgeons make medical advances in the health care of cats, the longevity of the typical house cat is improving. Certainly ages between 15 and 18 years are not uncommon, and reports of cats living more than 20 years are predictable.

A DELICATE HEART

A cat's heart is as delicate as a human's heart, but it is much smaller. At full maturity, a queen's heart weighs between 9–12 grammes. The tom's heart is heavier, weighing 11–18 grammes. The blood that circulates through the heart chambers does not supply the heart muscle, thus requiring a separate circulatory system for the heart muscle.

the amount given. The first vaccination is normally given when the kitten is about 8–9 weeks old. About 30 days later a booster is given. Although there are many diseases to which a cat may fall victim, the most dangerous three—FIE, FVR and FeLV—can be safeguarded against with a single (three-in-one) injection. Thereafter an annual booster is all that is required.

MAJOR DISEASES

There are a number of diseases for which there is either no cure or little chance of recovery. However, some can be prevented by vaccination. All breeders and owners should ensure kittens are so protected.

FELINE INFECTIOUS ENTERITIS (FIE)

This is also known as feline panleukopenia and feline distemper. The virus attacks the intestinal system. It is spread via

and you should keep a record of the date of the injection, the identification of the vaccine and

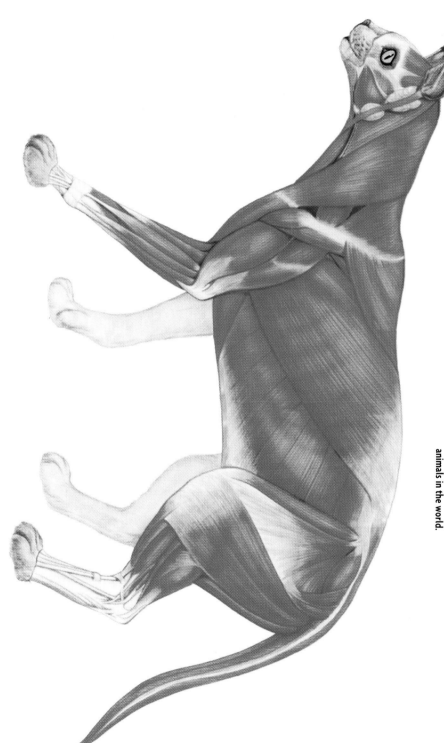

The cat's body consists of thousands of muscles, comprising a complex system that allows the domestic cat to be among the most flexible animals in the world.

the faeces and urine. The virus may survive for many years in some environments. The use of household bleach (sodium hypochlorite) for cleaning helps to prevent colonisation. Signs, among others, are diarrhoea, vomiting, depression, anorexia and dehydration. Death may occur within days. A vaccine is available from the vet.

FELINE VIRAL RHINOTRACHEITIS (FVR) & CALCIVIRUS (FCV)

Also known as cat flu, this is a complex of upper respiratory diseases. Signs are excessive hard sneezing, runny nose, and mouth ulcers. Cats vaccinated after having contracted flu may recover but may suffer recurrent bouts, especially if they become stressed.

FELINE LEUKAEMIA VIRUS (FeLV)

This is a highly infectious viral disease. It is spread via direct contact—mutual grooming, saliva, feeding bowls, faeces, urine and biting. It can be passed prenatally from a female to her offspring. It creates tumours, anaemia, immune system depression, pyrexia (high temperatures), lethargy, respiratory disease, intestinal disease and many other potentially fatal problems. It is most prevalent in high-density cat populations. Not all cats will be affected, but they may become carriers.

HEALTH AND VACCINATION SCHEDULE

AGE	6 WKS	8 WKS	10 WKS	12 WKS	16 WKS	6 MOS	1 YR
Worm control	✔	✔	✔		✔		
Neutering						✔	
Rhinotracheitis	✔	✔		✔	✔		✔
Panleukopenia	✔	✔		✔			✔
Calcivirus		✔			✔		✔
Feline Leukaemia				✔			✔
Feline Infectious Peritonitis				✔	✔		✔
Faecal evaluation					✔		
Feline Immunodeficiency testing							✔
Feline Leukaemia testing				✔			✔
Dental evaluation		✔				✔	
Rabies				✔	✔		✔

Vaccinations are not instantly effective. It takes about two weeks for the cat's immune system to develop antibodies. Most vaccinations require annual booster shots. Your veterinary surgeon should guide you in this regard.

DISEASE REFERENCE CHART

	What is it?	Cause	Symptoms
Feline Leukaemia Virus (FeLV)	Infectious disease; kills more cats each year than any other feline infectious disease.	A virus spread through saliva, tears, urine and faeces of infected cats; bite wounds.	Early on no symptoms may occur, but eventually infected cats experience signs from depression and weight loss to respiratory distress. FeLV also suppresses immune system, making a cat susceptible to almost any severe chronic illness.
Rabies	Potentially deadly virus that infects warm-blooded mammals.	A bacterium, often carried by rodents, that enters through mucous membranes and spreads quickly throughout the body.	Aggressiveness, a blank or vacant look in the eyes, increased vocalisation and/or weak or wobbly gait.
Feline Infectious Enteritis (FIE) aka Panleukopenia	Highly contagious virus, potentially deadly.	Ingestion of the virus, which is usually spread through the faeces of infected cats.	Most common: severe diarrhoea. Also vomiting, fatigue, lack of appetite, severe inflammation of intestines.
Feline Viral Rhinotracheitis (FVR)	Viral disease that affects eyes and upper respiratory tracts.	A virus that can affect any cat, especially those in multiple-cat settings.	Sneezing attacks, coughing, drooling thick saliva, fever, watery eyes, ulcers of mouth, nose and eyes.
Feline Immuno-deficiency Virus (FIV)	Virus that reduces white blood cells.	An infection spread commonly through cat-fight wounds.	Signs may be dormant for years or innocuous, such as diarrhoea or anaemia.
Feline Infectious Peritonitis (FIP)	A fatal viral disease, may be linked to FeLV and FIV.	Bacteria in dirty litter boxes; stress may increase susceptibility in kittens.	Extremely variable; range from abdominal swelling to chest problems, eye ailments and body lesions.
Feline Urological Syndrome (FUS)	A disease that affects the urinary tracts of cats.	Inflammation of bladder and urethra.	Constipation, constant licking of penis or vulva, blood in urine (males), swollen abdomen, crying when lifted.

Kittens less than six months old are especially vulnerable. Infected cats usually die by the time they are three to four years old. Cats can be screened or tested for this disease. Vaccination is not 100% effective but is recommended in kittens being sold into multi-cat environments.

FELINE IMMUNODEFICIENCY VIRUS (FIV)

This causes the white blood cells to be significantly reduced, thus greatly suppressing the efficiency of the immune system. It is not transferable to humans. Infection is normally gained from cat fight wounds; thus, outdoor males are at the most risk. A cat diagnosed via blood tests as FIV positive may live a normal life for months or years if retained indoors and given careful attention. Signs may be innocuous in the early stages, such as anaemia or diarrhoea. No vaccine is available.

KEEPING YOUR CAT HEALTHY

Although there are a multitude of ailments, diseases and accidents that could befall a cat, all but the most minor of problems can be avoided with good management. The following tips are a recipe for keeping your cat in the peak of health.

- Make sure it is vaccinated and in other ways protected from each of the major diseases. It must also receive annual boosters to maintain immunity.
- Have periodic checks made by your vet to see if your cat has worms.
- Ensure the cat receives an adequate diet that is both appealing and balanced.
- Have the kitten neutered if it is not to be used for breeding.
- Ensure the cat's litter tray, food/water vessels and grooming tools are always maintained in spotless condition.
- Do not let your cat out overnight or when you are away working or shopping.
- Always wash your hands after gardening or petting other people's pets.
- Groom your cat daily. If this is done, you will more readily notice fleas or other problems than if grooming was done less frequently.
- Never try to diagnose and treat problems that are clearly of an internal type. Remember, even the most informed of breeders is not a vet and unable to reliably diagnose problems for you or advise treatments. Contact your vet.
- If you are ever in doubt about the health of your cat, do not delay in discussing your concerns with your vet. Delays merely allow problems to become more established.

FELINE INFECTIOUS PERITONITIS (FIP)

This viral disease is invariably fatal once contracted in its more potent forms. However, the virulence of the virus is variable and may by destroyed by the immune system. Stress may increase susceptibility in kittens. It may be linked to FeLV and FIV. Signs are extremely variable and range from abdominal swelling to chest problems, eye ailments to body lesions. There are various tests available but none is as yet 100% conclusive. Strict cleanliness is essential, especially of litter trays. No vaccine is available.

FELINE UROLOGICAL SYNDROME (FUS)

This is a very distressing condition caused by an inflammation of the bladder and urethra. Signs are constipation-like squatting and attempts to urinate, regular licking of the penis or vulva, blood in urine (males), swollen abdomen, crying when lifted and urinating in unusual places (often with only small amounts).

The numerous causes include infection, dirty litter tray of the indoor cat, alkaline urine (in cats it should be acidic), diet too dry, lack of water intake (even though

this may be available) and being hit by vehicle (damaged nerves). Veterinary treatment is essential

NEUTERING

Neutering is a major means of avoiding ill health. It dramatically reduces the risk of males' becoming involved in territorial battles with the dangers of physical injury and disease transference. It makes the male more placid and less likely to scent mark its home. It also reduces the incidence of prostate problems, and there is no risk of testicular cancer. The female avoids potentially lethal illnesses related to her being allowed to remain in an unmated condition, such as breast cancer.

Neutering is usually performed between four and six months of age, but it can be done as early as eight weeks of age. Data available on the age at which a kitten is neutered indicate that early neutering has more advantages than drawbacks. Breeders should have this performed on all cats sold as pets.

Male cats are neutered. The operation removes the testicles and requires that the cat be anaesthetised. Females are spayed. This is major surgery during which the ovaries and uterus are removed. Both males and females should be kept quiet at home for about seven to ten days following the procedure, at which time the vet will remove the sutures.

CLEANLINESS IS THE KEY

Crucial to the prevention and spread of disease is the need to maintain meticulous cleanliness, especially relating to the litter tray. Many diseases and problems are transferred via faecal matter. Once a problem is suspected, the advice of a vet should be sought. Blood tests, faecal microscopy and other testing methods are now available. They can mean the difference between life and death of a cherished pet.

or the condition could be fatal due to the bladder's bursting or presence of dangerous bacteria.

RABIES

Britain and most European Community countries are free of this terrible disease. The stringent quarantine laws of Britain are such that vaccination is not necessary. However, the introduction of passports for dogs and cats means that resident British cats must be vaccinated if they are to travel abroad and return to the UK without being placed into quarantine. The vaccination is given when the kitten is three or more months old. The pet passport process takes at least six months to complete, so plan well ahead.

COMMON HEALTH PROBLEMS

Dermatitis (Eczema)

Dry lifeless coat, loss of coat, tiny scabs over the head and body, loose flakes (dandruff) and excessive scratching are all commonly called eczema. The

HEALTHY CAT

The enormous population of pet cats has stimulated the veterinary medical community to learn more about cats and to develop more modern medicines to keep felines healthier.

Water is a basic requirement of every living creature, and most Bengals love a noisy faucet. Here is Topspot Asia helping herself to a little refreshment. Owners, Charles and Mary McGee.

cause covers a range of possibilities including diet, parasitic mites such as *Cheyletiella spp*, fungus or an allergy to flea or other bites. Sometimes reasons are unknown. Veterinary diagnosis and treatment are required.

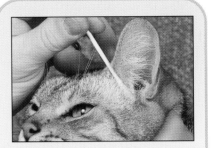

POSSIBLE SOURCES OF EAR PROBLEMS

- Fight scratches
- Excess secretion of wax
- Swellings and blood blisters (haematoma) resulting from intrusion by foreign bodies (grass, etc.)
- Sunburn
- Whitish-coloured ear mites (*Otodectes cynotis*)
- Orange-coloured harvest mites (*Trombicula autumnalis*)
- Fleas
- Bacterial infection of either the outer or middle/inner ear

RINGWORM (*DERMATOPHYTOSIS*)

This problem is fungal, not that of a worm. The most common form is *Microsporum canis*, which accounts for over 90% of cases. Cats less than one year old are at the highest risk, while longhaired breeds are more prone to the problem than shorthaired cats. The fungi feed on the keratin layers of the skin, nails and hair. Direct contact and spores that remain in the environment are the main means of transmission.

Typical signs are circular-type bald areas of skin, which may be flaked and reddish. The coat generally may become dry and lifeless, giving the appearance of numerous other skin and hair problems. Veterinary diagnosis and treatment, either topical or via drugs, is essential as the condition is zoonotic. This means it can be transferred to humans.

EAR PROBLEMS

Most of the common ear problems affect the outer ear. Recognition is by the cat's constant scratching of the ears and/or its holding the ear to one side. Greasy hairs around the ear, dark brown wax (cerumen) in the ears, scaly flakes in or around the ear or minute white or orange pinhead-like bodies (mites) in the ear are common signs. Canker is a term used for ear infections, but it has no specific meaning.

Over-the-counter remedies for ear problems are ineffective unless correct diagnosis has been made. It is therefore better to let the vet diagnose and treat the cat. Some problems may require anaesthesia and minor surgery.

DIARRHOEA

This is a general term used to indicate a semi-liquid to liquid state of faecal matter. Mild to acute cases may be due to a change of home, dietary change,

eating an 'off' item, gorging on a favoured food, stress or a minor chill. These often rectify themselves within days. Chronic and persistent diarrhoea may be

THE RIB CAGE

Cats usually have 13 pairs of ribs. The ribs in the middle are longer than the ribs on either end (or beginning) of the rib cage. The first nine ribs are joined to the chest bone (sternum) with costal cartilages. Ribs 10, 11 and 12 are also associated with cartilage, which contributes to the costal arch. The thirteenth rib is called the floating rib and its cartilage is separate from the other ribs.

CONSTIPATION

When a cat strains but is unable to pass motions, this is indicative of many causes. It may have hairballs, may have eaten a bird or rodent and has a bone lodged in its intestinal tract, may be suffering from a urological problem rather than constipation, or may have been hit by a car and has damaged the nerves that control bowel movements. As constipation is potentially serious, veterinary advice should be sought. Laxatives and faecal softener tablets may be given, the faecal matter can be surgically removed or other treatment carried out.

Bengals have medium-sized ears with a wide base, sometimes with furnishings inside. Monitor the cleanliness of your Bengal's ears regularly. This wide-eyed beauty is Topspot Jazzman, a most affectionate and healthy tom. Owner, Andrew De Prisco.

the result of specific diseases. Any indication of blood in the faecal matter must be considered dangerous.

In minor cases, withholding food for 12–24 hours, or feeding a simple diet, may arrest the condition. If not, wisdom suggests contacting your vet. Faecal analysis and blood testing may be required. By asking numerous questions related to the cat's diet, general health, level of activity, loss of appetite, etc., the vet will determine whether tests are required or if immediate treatment seems more appropriate. Do not give cats human or canine intestinal remedies; these could prove dangerous.

STRESS TEST

Stress reduces the effectiveness of the immune system. Seemingly innocuous conditions may develop into major problems or leave the cat more open to attack by disease. Stress is difficult to specifically identify, but its major causes are well known. These include incorrect diet, intrusion by another cat in its home or territory, excessive handling and petting, disturbed sleep, uncomfortable home temperatures, bullying by another cat or pet, parasitic infestation, boarding in a cattery, travel, moving, boredom, limited accommodation space and, for some felines, being exhibited.

EXTERNAL PARASITES

FLEAS

Of all the problems to which cats are prone, none is more well known and frustrating than fleas. Indeed, flea-related problems are the principal cause of visits to veterinary surgeons. Flea infestation is relatively simple to cure but difficult to prevent. Periodic flea checks for your cat, conducted as well as annual health check-ups, are highly recommended. Consistent dosing with anthelmintic preparations is also advised. Parasites that are harboured inside the body are a bit more difficult to eradicate, but they are easier to control.

To control a flea infestation, you have to understand the flea's life cycle. Fleas are often thought of as a summertime problem but centrally heated homes have changed the life-cycle patterns, and fleas can be found at any time of the year. Fleas thrive in hot and humid environments; they soon die if the temperature drops below 2°C (35°F). The most effective method of flea control is a two-stage approach: one stage to kill the adult fleas, and the other to control the development of pre-adult fleas. Unfortunately, no single active ingredient is effective against all stages of the life cycle.

Flea prevention is a challenge to cat owners in most places. This is an adult male flea.

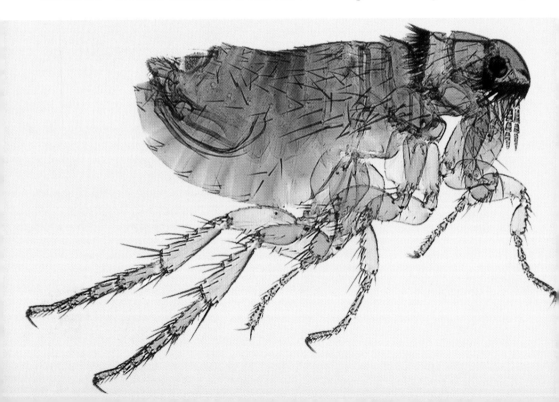

A Look at Fleas

Fleas have been around for millions of years and have adapted to changing host animals. They are able to go through a complete life cycle in less than one month, or they can extend their lives to almost two years by remaining as pupae or cocoons. They must have a blood meal every 10-14 days, and egg production begins within 2 days of their first meal. The female cat flea is very prolific and can lay 2000 eggs in her lifetime!

Fleas have been measured as being able to jump 300,000 times and can jump 150 times their body length in any direction, including straight up. Those are just a few of the reasons why they are so successful in infesting a cat!

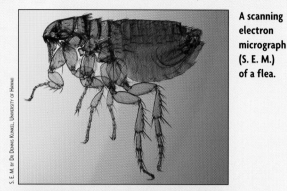

A scanning electron micrograph (S. E. M.) of a flea.

Magnified head of a flea.

LIFE CYCLE STAGES

During its life, a flea will pass through four life stages: egg, larva, pupa and adult. The adult stage is the most visible and irritating stage of the flea life cycle, and this is why the majority of flea-control products concentrate on this stage. The fact is that adult fleas account for only 1% of the total flea population, and the other 99% exist in pre-adult stages, i.e. eggs, larvae and pupae. The pre-adult stages are barely visible to the naked eye.

THE LIFE CYCLE OF THE FLEA

Eggs are laid on the cat, usually in quantities of about 20 or 30, several times a day. The female adult flea must have a blood meal before each egg-laying session. When first laid, the eggs will not cling to the cat's fur, as the eggs are not sticky. They will immediately fall to the floor or ground, especially when the cat moves around or scratches.

Once the eggs fall from the cat onto the carpet or grass, they will hatch into yellow larvae, approximately 2 mms long. This takes from 5 to 11 days. Larvae are not particularly mobile and will usually travel only a few inches from where they hatch. However, they do have a tendency to move away from light and heavy traffic—under furniture, in the carpet and behind doors are common places to find high quantities of flea larvae.

The flea larvae feed on dead organic matter, including adult flea faeces, until they are ready to change into adult fleas. Fleas will usually remain as larvae for around seven days, becoming darker in colour. After this period, the larvae will pupate a protective cocoon. While inside the pupae, the larvae will undergo metamorphosis and change into adult fleas. This can happen within a week, but the adult fleas can remain inside the pupae waiting to hatch for up to six months. The pupae are signalled to hatch by certain stimuli, such as physical pressure—the pupae's being stepped on, heat from an animal lying on the pupae or increased

Opposite page: A scanning electron micrograph of a flea, magnified more than 100x. This image has been colorized for effect.

> **DID YOU KNOW?**
> Never mix flea-control products without first consulting your veterinary surgeon. Some products can become toxic when combined with others and can cause serious or fatal consequences.

> **DID YOU KNOW?**
> Flea-killers are poisonous. You should not spray these toxic chemicals on areas of a cat's body that he licks, on his genitals or on his face. Flea killers taken internally are a better answer, but check with your vet in case internal therapy is not advised for your cat.

carbon dioxide levels and vibrations—indicating that a suitable host is available.

Once hatched, the adult flea must feed within a few days. Once the adult flea finds a host, it will not leave voluntarily. It only becomes dislodged by grooming or the host animal's scratching. The adult flea will remain on the host for the duration of its life unless forcibly removed.

TREATING THE ENVIRONMENT AND THE CAT

Treating fleas should be a two-pronged attack. First, the environment needs to be treated; this includes carpets and furniture, especially the cat's bedding and areas underneath furniture. The environment should be treated with a household spray containing an Insect Growth Regulator (IGR) and an insecticide to kill the adult fleas. There are also liquids, given orally, that contain chitin inhibitors. These

A brown tick, *Rhipicephalus sanguineus*, is an uncommon but annoying tick found on cats.

render flea eggs incapable of development. There are also both foam and liquid wipe-on treatments. Additionally, cats can be injected with treatments that can last up to six months. Emulsions that have the same effect can also be added to food. The advanced treatments are only available from veterinary surgeons. The IGRs actually mimic the fleas' own hormones and stop the eggs and larvae from developing into adult fleas. There are currently no treatments available to attack the pupa stage of the life cycle, so the adult insecticide is used to kill the newly hatched adult fleas before they find a host. Most IGRs are active for many months, while adult insecticides are only active for a few days.

The head of a tick, *Dermacentor variabilis*, enlarged and coloured for effect.

When treating with a household spray, it is a good idea to vacuum before applying the product. This stimulates as many pupae as possible to hatch into adult fleas. The vacuum cleaner should also be treated with a flea

Dwight R Kuhn's magnificent action photo, showing a flea jumping.

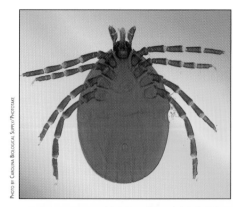

PHOTO BY CAROLINA BIOLOGICAL SUPPLY/PHOTOTAKE

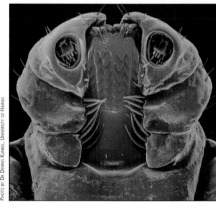

PHOTO BY DR DENNIS KUNKEL, UNIVERSITY OF HAWAII

treatment to prevent the eggs and larvae that have been hoovered into the vacuum bag from hatching.

The second stage of treatment is to apply an adult insecticide to the cat, usually in the form of a collar or a spray. Alternatively, there are drops that, when placed on the back of the animal's neck, spread throughout the fur and skin to kill adult fleas. A word of warning: Never use products sold for dogs on your cat; the result could be fatal.

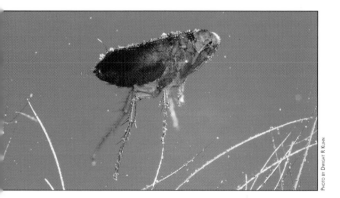

PHOTO BY DWIGHT R KUHN

The Life Cycle of the Flea

Eggs

Larvae

Pupa

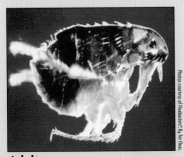

Adult

Photos courtesy of Fleabusters®, Rx for Fleas.

Flea Control

IGR (INSECT GROWTH REGULATOR)

Two types of products should be used when treating fleas—a product to treat the pet and a product to treat the home. Adult fleas represent 1% of the flea population. The pre-adult fleas (eggs, larvae and pupae) represent 99% of the flea population and are found in the environment; it is in the case of pre-adult fleas that products containing an Insect Growth Regulator (IGR) should be used in the home.

IGRs are a new class of compounds used to prevent the development of insects. They do not kill the insect outright, but instead use the insect's biology against it to stop it from completing its growth. Products that contain methoprene are the world's first and leading IGRs. Used to control fleas and other insects, this type of IGR will stop flea larvae from developing and protect the house for up to seven months.

EN GARDE:
CATCHING FLEAS OFF GUARD!

Consider the following ways to arm yourself against fleas:

• Add a small amount of pennyroyal or eucalyptus oil to your cat's bath. These natural remedies repel fleas.

• Supplement your cat's food with fresh garlic (minced or grated) and a hearty amount of brewer's yeast, both of which ward off fleas.

• Use a flea comb on your cat daily. Submerge fleas in a cup of bleach to kill them quickly.

• Confine the cat to only a few rooms to limit the spread of fleas in the home.

• Vacuum daily...and get all of the crevices! Dispose of the bag every few days until the problem is under control.

• Wash your cat's bedding daily. Cover cushions where your cat sleeps with towels, and wash the towels often.

Opposite page:
The tick,
Dermacentor
variabilis, is one
of the most
common ticks
found on cats.
Look at the
strength in its
eight legs! No
wonder it's hard
to detach them.

TICKS AND MITES

Though not as common as fleas, ticks and mites are found all over the tropical and temperate world. They don't bite like fleas; they harpoon. They dig their sharp proboscis (nose) into the cat's skin and drink the blood. Their only food and drink is your cat's blood. Cats can get potentially fatal anaemia, paralysis and many other diseases from ticks and mites. They may live where fleas are found and they like to hide in cracks or seams in walls wherever cats live. They are controlled the same way fleas are controlled.

The *Dermacentor variabilis* may well be the most common tick in many geographical areas, especially those areas where the climate is hot and humid. The other common ticks that attack small animals are *Rhipicephalus sanguineus*, *Ixodes* and some species of *Amblyomma*.

Most ticks have life expectancies of a week to six months, depending upon climatic conditions. They can neither jump nor fly, but they can crawl slowly and can range up to 5 metres (16 feet) to reach a sleeping or unsuspecting animal.

INTERNAL PARASITES

Most animals—fishes, birds and mammals, including cats and humans—have worms and other parasites that live inside their bodies. According to Dr Herbert R Axelrod, the fish pathologist, there are two kinds of parasites: dumb and smart. The smart parasites live in peaceful cooperation with their hosts (symbiosis), while the dumb parasites kill their hosts. Most of the worm infections are relatively

TOXOPLASMOSIS AND PREGNANT WOMEN

Toxoplasmosis is caused by a single parasite, *Toxoplasma gondii*. Cats acquire it by eating infected prey, such as rodents or birds, or raw meat. Obviously, strictly indoor cats are at less risk of infection than cats that are permitted to roam outdoors. Symptoms include diarrhoea, listlessness, pneumonia and inflammation of the eye. Sometimes there are no symptoms. The disease can be treated with antibiotics.

The only way humans can get the disease is through direct contact with the cat's faeces. People usually don't display any symptoms, although they can show mild flu-like symptoms. Once exposed, an antibody is produced and the person builds immunity to the disease.

The real danger to humans is that pregnant women can pass the parasite to the developing foetus. In this case the chances are good that the baby will be born with a major health problem and/or serious birth defects. In order to eliminate risk, pregnant women should have someone else deal with the litter-box duties or wear gloves while taking care of the litter box and wash hands thoroughly afterwards.

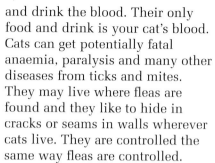

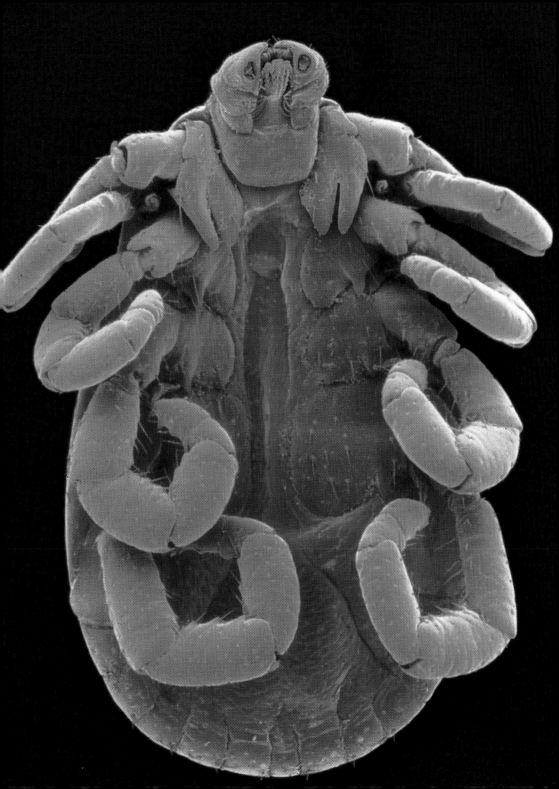

easy to control. If they are not controlled, they weaken the host cat to the point that other medical problems occur, but they are not dumb parasites.

HOOKWORMS

The worm *Ancylostoma tubaeforme* can infect a cat by larva penetrating its skin. It attaches itself to the small intestine of the cat, where it sucks blood. This loss of blood could cause iron-deficiency anaemia.

Outdoor cats that spend much of their time in the garden or in contact with soil are commonly infected with hookworm. There is another worm, the *Gordius* or horsehair worm, that, if ingested by a cat, causes vomiting.

TAPEWORMS

There are many species of tapeworms. They are carried by

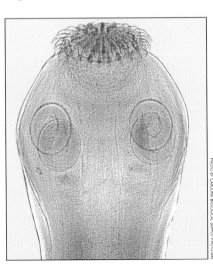

The head and rostellum (the round prominence on the scolex) of a tapeworm, which infects cats and humans.

PHOTO BY CAROLINA BIOLOGICAL SUPPLY/PHOTOTAKE

fleas! The cat eats the flea and starts the tapeworm cycle. Humans can also be infected with tapeworms, so don't eat fleas! Fleas are so small that your cat could pass them onto your hands, your plate or your food and thus make it possible for you to ingest a flea that is carrying tapeworm eggs.

While tapeworm infection is not life-threatening in cats (smart parasite!), it can be the cause of a

INTERNAL PARASITES OF CATS

NAME	DESCRIPTION	SYMPTOMS	ACQUISITION	TREATMENT
Roundworm (*Toxocara cati* and *Toxascaris leonina*)	Large, white, coil-like worms, 5–10 cms (2–4 inches) long, resembling small springs.	Vomiting, pot belly, respiratory problems, poor growth rate, protruding third eyelids, poor haircoat.	Ingesting infective larvae; ingesting infected mammals, birds or insects; a queen with *Toxocari cati* nursing kittens.	Anthelmintics; scrupulously clean environment (e.g. daily removal of all faeces recommended).
***Physaloptera* species**	2–15 cms (1–6 inches) long, attacks the wall of the stomach.	Vomiting, anorexia, melena.	Eating insects that live in soil (e.g. May beetles).	Diagnosed with a gastroscope; treated with pyrantel pamoate. Prevention of exposure to the intermediate hosts.
***Gordius* or Horsehair worm**	15-cms (6-inch) pale brown worms with stripes.	Vomiting.	May ingest a worm while drinking from or making contact with swimming pools and toilet bowls.	Anthelmintics; avoiding potentially infected environments.
Hookworm (*Ancylostoma tubaeforme*)	The adult worms, ranging from 6 to 15 mms (2.5–6 inches) in length, attach themselves to the small intestines.	Anaemia, melena, weight loss, poor haircoat.	Larva penetrating the cat's skin, usually attacks the small intestine. Found in soil and flower gardens where faecal matter is deposited.	Fortnightly treatment with anthelmintics. Good sanitation (e.g. daily cleanup of litter boxes).
Tapeworm (*Dipylidium caninum* and *Taenia taeniformis*)	Up to 91 cms (3 feet) long. Parts shaped similar to cucumber seeds. The most common intermediate hosts are fleas and biting lice.	No clinical signs— difficult to detect.	Eating infected adult fleas. Uses rodents as hosts.	Praziquantel and epsiprantel. Management of environment to ensure scrupulously clean conditions. Proper flea control.

Magnified heartworm larvae, *Dirofilaria immitis.*

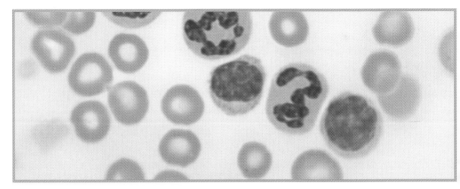

The heartworm, *Dirofilaria immitis.*

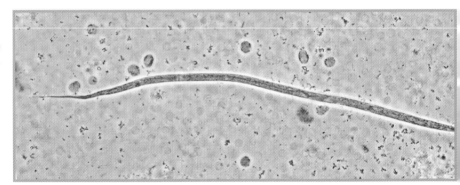

very serious liver disease for humans. About 50 percent of the humans infected with *Echinococcus multilocularis*, a type of tapeworm that causes alveolar hydatis, perish.

HEARTWORMS

Heartworms are thin, extended worms up to 30 cms (12 ins) long, which are difficult to diagnose in cats as the worms are too few to be identified by the antigen-detection test. Symptoms may be loss of energy, loss of appetite, coughing, the development of a potbelly and anaemia. Heartworm infection in cats should be treated very seriously, as it is often fatal.

Heartworms are transmitted by mosquitoes. The mosquito drinks the blood of an infected cat and takes in larvae with the blood. It takes two to three weeks for the larvae to develop to the infective stage within the body of the mosquito. Cats are less frequently infected with heartworms than dogs are. Also, the parasite is more likely to attack the cat's brain or other organs rather than the heart. Cats should be treated at about six weeks of age, and maintained on a prophylactic dose given monthly.

THE FELINE EYE

by Lorraine Waters BvetNed, CertVOphthal, MRCVS

This part of the book aims to provide an owner's guide to feline ophthalmology, the study of eyes, which is an area of increasing concern for cat owners.

Eye diseases in the cat usually result from trauma, infection or neoplasia. Unlike the dog, the cat has few inherited eye conditions. Most of the conditions to be discussed are not amenable to first-aid measures or home remedies. Therefore, if you are at all worried about your cat's eyes, you should seek prompt veterinary attention.

Ocular pain is frequently associated with eye disease and can be recognised in your cat because it will show a combination of the following signs:

blinking, increased tear production, fear of light and rubbing at the eye. Some conditions result in loss of vision; a gradual loss of vision may go unnoticed, as the cat slowly adapts, but a sudden loss produces an obvious change in behaviour. Being blind may not be as bad as it sounds, as cats adapt and cope amazingly well in familiar surroundings.

To examine the eye properly, veterinary surgeons first use a bright light, which allows close examination of the lids, conjunctiva, cornea and iris. Following this, an ophthalmoscope can be used, in a darkened room, to give a magnified view. Then, by using the lenses within the ophthalmoscope, it is possible to focus on the structures further back in the eye, such as the lens, vitreous and retina.

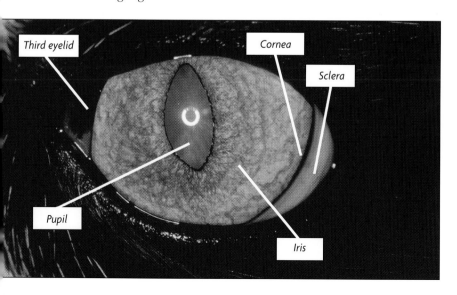

Third eyelid

Cornea

Sclera

Pupil

Iris

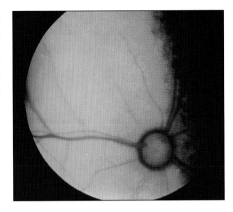

The feline fundus, the eye as seen through the veterinary surgeon's ophthalmoscope.

DISEASES OF THE FELINE EYE

GLOBE AND ORBIT

The eye sits in a bony socket in the skull known as the orbit. In short-nosed breeds, the orbit is shallow and the normal-sized eyes bulge forward. This situation can predispose a number of problems, such as exposure keratitis, overflow of tears and even prolapse of the globe (eye). Cats can be born with eyes that are too small and sink back into the orbit, to be covered by the third eyelid. This is non-inherited and usually associated with damage to the eye in utero. Abnormal enlargement of the globe may be congenital, buphthalmos, or acquired, hydrophthalmos, and is the end point of glaucoma.

The globe can prolapse from the orbit following head trauma, a common injury for cats involved in road traffic accidents. A minor prolapse replaced early can result in restoration of normal function. However, there is often stretching of the optic nerve and tearing of the extra-ocular muscles. In these cases the eye may be permanently damaged and have to be surgically removed. As an emergency measure, applying a moist cloth to the prolapsed eye on the way to the surgery will help preserve it.

Problems behind the eye become evident when they cause the eye to bulge forward along with the third eyelid. These include tooth root abscesses, foreign bodies, tumours and occasionally haemorrhage.

EYELIDS

The eyes of a kitten should open around 10–14 days of age. Once this has occurred, it is possible to see if the lids have been properly formed. Failure of all or part of the eyelids to develop is a rare congen-

EYE DROPS

Topical ointments and drops are often prescribed for the treatment of eye disease. There are a few simple rules to follow when administering them. It is important to clean away discharges before applying treatment. Only give one drop or just a few millimetres of ointment; if you give too much, it will be diluted by increased tear production. Systemic drugs are those given by mouth to achieve higher concentrations at the back of the eye or for diseases which involve other body systems.

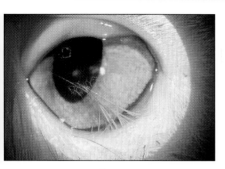

Eyelid coloboma is a rare congenital problem in cats.

ital problem, known as coloboma. The unprotected cornea, in the affected area, may become damaged and the lid must be surgically restored. Early infection in the eye may delay or prevent eyelid opening; the lids can be opened surgically to allow bathing and appropriate medication to be given.

Entropion and ectropion are common conditions in the dog and are related to conformation. Fortunately these are rare in cats and can be surgically corrected. Entropion secondary to ocular pain may remain once the cause of the pain is removed. Fortunately these cases will respond to corrective surgery. Extra or abnormally positioned hairs are frequently seen as an inherited problem in dogs, but are rare in cats.

There are several types of tumours that can occur on the eyelids. The most common type is squamous cell carcinoma, more prevalent in white and part-white cats, as ultra-violet light (sunlight) plays a role in causing this condition. Treatment may consist

of cryotherapy, surgical excision or radiation treatment. Early recognition and treatment are essential to prevent destructive local spreading.

CONJUNCTIVA

The pink tissue lining the eyelid and covering the third eyelid and front of the sclera is called conjunctiva. Dermoids are elements of skin tissue that arise in abnormal places. Dermoids often, but not invariably, contain hairs and can form on the conjunctiva and/or cornea. Dermoids act as foreign bodies in the eye, causing irritation and pain, and need to be surgically removed.

The most frequently encountered problem with the conjunctiva is conjunctivitis. In cats the majority of cases are infectious. An eye with conjunctivitis usually looks red and swollen with signs of ocular pain. Discharges may be watery or sticky yellow, indicating bacterial infection.

The most common infectious cause of feline conjunctivitis is feline herpesvirus (FHV). Feline calicivirus (FCV) can also cause

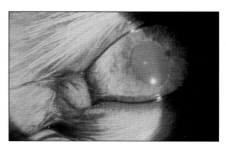

Dermoid in a longhaired cat can cause conjunctiva.

Conjunctivitis, frequently an infectious disease in cats.

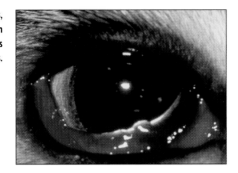

conjunctivitis and is usually associated with other problems, such as upper respiratory tract signs and mouth ulcers. The bacteria *Chlamydia psittaci* can cause conjunctivitis in individual cats and in multi-cat households. Individual cases respond well to appropriate antibiotic therapy. Chronic and recurrent conjunctivitis in multi-cat situations requires thorough and prolonged treatment, management changes and, where appropriate, vaccination. *Mycoplasma spp.* can cause a less severe conjunctivitis than *Chlamydia spp.* Opportunistic infection can occur following cat-fight wounds, as bacteria are found on cats' teeth and claws.

Corneal ulcer stained with fluorescein.

Tear staining is more commonly seen in short-nosed cat breeds.

Non-infectious causes of conjunctivitis include trauma, foreign bodies, allergic disease, tumours and pre-corneal tear film abnormalities. Eosinophilic kerato-conjunctivitis is a disease in which the conjunctiva and cornea are invaded by cells from the immune system, primarily mast cells and eosinophils. These cells are responsible for inflammation and allergic reactions. This tends to occur in young to middle-aged cats and may

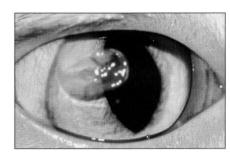

be seasonal. Treatment usually works well but may be required long-term.

Several forms of neoplasia (cancer) can affect the conjunctiva in cats and can be either primary tumours arising in the conjunctiva or secondary, spreading from elsewhere in the body.

SCLERA

The sclera is the white fibrous coat of the globe. It is partially covered by conjunctiva and protects the more fragile internal structures. Congenital defects of this structure are very rare. Inflammation

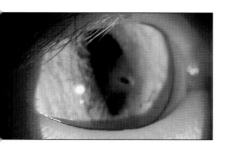

Tear staining is also seen in short-nosed breeds because the duct is tortuous and drainage inadequate. This is also associated with medial lower lid entropion, occluding the duct opening. This anatomical combination is very difficult to improve surgically.

(scleritis and episcleritis) is a problem in dogs and humans but is extremely rare in cats. Feline scleral diseases are usually associated with trauma and neoplasia.

PRE-CORNEAL TEAR FILM

This forms from tears and moistens, lubricates and helps protect the cornea. Decreased tear production occurs if the tear glands are not working properly and results in a condition called 'dry eye' or keratoconjunctivis sicca (KCS). The cornea becomes dry and roughened leading to keratitis and ulceration. It can occur following feline herpesvirus (FHV) infection, trauma, facial paralysis and chronic inflammation.

Overproduction of tears can be seen as a result of ocular pain. The naso-lacrimal duct drains the tears; it runs from the inner corner of the eye to just inside the end of the nose. Congenital defects, such as a small duct opening, result in tear overflow and staining around the eye. These can usually be corrected surgically. Acquired blockages may result from chronic conjunctivitis or foreign bodies.

CORNEA

The cornea is the clear circular area at the front of the eye through which the iris and pupil can be seen. Light passes through and is focused by the cornea, before passing through the lens and hence onto the retina. Congenital defects are rare but include micro- and megalocornea. There is sometimes a transient cloudiness following opening of the eyes but it should disappear by four weeks of age.

One of the most common problems involving the cornea is ulceration, where the top layer of corneal cells (the epithelium) is lost and the nerve endings exposed, resulting in ocular pain. Fluorescein is a special stain that

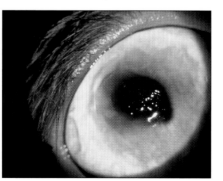

Corneal sequestrum.

Symblepharon, adhesion of the eyelid to the eyeball.

can be used to reveal ulcers; they show up as a yellow/green patch on the cornea. If your cat has had this performed, you may have noticed the stain appearing at the end of its nose; this is because it drains down the naso-lacrimal duct and demonstrates that it is not blocked.

The most common cause of ulceration is trauma, from fight wounds or foreign bodies. FHV can cause ulceration. There is also a form of ulceration where the epithelium does not stick down again after healing and can easily become detached. This is seen as a breed-related problem in dogs. In cats it can be seen in older animals or associated with FHV infection, resulting in recurrent ulcer formation.

The cornea is very quick to repair ulcers and, provided that the initial cause is removed, healing should only take a few days. Antibiotics are often applied to the eye while ulcers heal to prevent bacterial infection. Ulcers need

prompt veterinary attention as they can deteriorate rapidly; deep ulcers can lead to rupture of the eye and require urgent surgical repair.

The cornea is a common site for cat scratch injuries and some may even penetrate the full thickness into the anterior chamber. If these wounds are repaired quickly and appropriate medical therapy is used, vision can usually be preserved. More severe ones may require reconstructive surgery, removal of the lens or even surgical removal of the eye.

Corneal foreign bodies usually result in ocular pain and need to be removed. Non-painful ones also need to be removed as they may penetrate the eye, causing internal problems.

Corneal sequestrum or necrosis is a condition specific to cats. The corneal stroma (middle layer) degenerates, turns brown/black and emerges through the epithelium, causing ulceration and a foreign body reaction with signs of ocular pain. These lesions usually need to be removed surgically because of the discomfort they cause, but a few will slough off naturally. Often a sequestrum will recur in the same eye or occur in the opposite eye at a later date. This condition is most commonly seen in Colourpoint Persians and is thought to have an inherited component. It may be related to their prominent eye position. The next most common breed with sequestra is the Burmese.

Following healing of a corneal wound, there is usually formation of a scar, which shows up as a white mark, but unless scars are extensive, they do not usually affect vision.

FHV-related Eye Diseases

A combination of treatments is often required to treat feline herpesvirus (FHV) infection. In acute case, kittens are often very sick and need supportive treatment and intensive nursing. Systemic and topical antibiotics are used, sometimes in combination with topical antiviral drugs. Cats that develop symblepharon after acute infection may be blinded by the condition and require new reconstructive surgical techniques. The chronic cases can be difficult to diagnose and challenging to treat. Topical antivirals can be used and in non-ulcerated cases combined with corticosteroids. More recent treatments include L-lysine (to inhibit viral replication), Cimetidine and alpha-interferon (to boost the local immune response).

The reason for chronic FHV disease is that individuals become carriers of the virus. When they are stressed, the virus is reactivated and signs of infection and the cat's immune response to it manifest in the eye. This can be a major problem in multi-cat households, with carrier animals infecting kittens and adults alike. In these cases, management changes, including the identification of carriers, use of early vaccinations and isolation of new arrivals, must be instituted.

Aqueous Humour

The aqueous humour is a watery fluid that is responsible for maintaining pressure within the eye. If the drainage angle is blocked and aqueous cannot drain away, pressure within the eye builds up, causing glaucoma. Glaucoma due to a congenitally obstructed drainage system is an inherited problem in many breeds of dog but is rare in the cat. When glaucoma does occur in cats, it is usually acquired, with drainage blocked by inflammatory or neoplastic cells.

Anterior uveitis can result in white blood cells in the anterior chamber, which gives it a cloudy look known as aqueous flare. Infection following penetrating wounds can result in pus accumulating in the chamber, known as hypopyon. Trauma to the eye and intra-ocular tumours may lead to bleeding into the anterior chamber

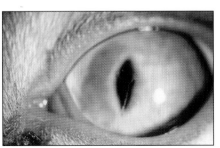

Herpesvirus ulcer.

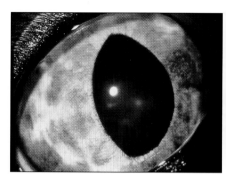

Iris pigment change in an old cat.

(space behind the cornea and in front of the iris), known as hyphaema. This blood usually forms a clot and is absorbed. Foreign bodies can also occasionally be seen in the anterior chamber.

IRIS AND CILIARY BODY

The iris and ciliary body are muscular and vascular structures that lie behind the cornea and in front of the lens. The iris is pigmented and gives the cat's eye its colour. Congenital defects are rare, but occasionally cats are born with pieces of the iris missing. Changes in iris colour can occur for a number of reasons; as young cats mature, their iris colour may deepen. Inflammation results in reddening of the iris, due to an increase in blood vessel formation and engorgement, and is known as rubeosis iridis. Following inflammation, the iris can remain permanently dark. As cats age they can develop a condition called melanosis. This is usually but not always a diffuse change, occurring

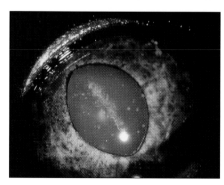

Iris melanoma, exhibited as a tumour of pigment cells that results in discoloration of the iris.

slowly in both eyes. It must be monitored and differentiated from iris melanoma. Melanoma is a tumour of the pigment cells that can result in either diffuse or nodular discoloration of the iris. It usually progresses quickly and only in one eye. This type of neoplasia has a potential to spread outside the eye and is usually treated by surgically removing the affected eye.

A difference in colour between the two irises is known as heterochromia iridis and can occur naturally in white or poorly pigmented breeds, usually associated with congenital deafness. In other cats, it usually indicates a problem in one eye or the other.

The ciliary body and iris are known as the anterior uvea, while the choroid (the vascular layer that lies between the retina and the sclera and provides a blood supply to the retina) is the posterior uvea. Uveitis is an inflammation of the uvea. It may involve both the anterior and posterior uvea and has many causes in the cat. The main

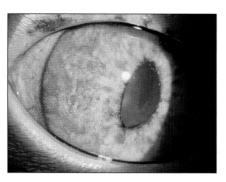

infectious causes are feline immunodeficiency virus (FIV), feline leukaemia virus (FeLV), feline infectious peritonitis (FIP) and toxoplasmosis. Tuberculosis has been reported in cats as a cause of uveitis and in sub-tropical and tropical countries fungal infection can be a significant cause. The signs of uveitis, for all these diseases are very similar and may include a constricted pupil, rubeosis iridis, aqueous flare, poor vision and ocular pain. It can be difficult to determine the cause in some cases despite thorough investigation. Even if the primary viral infection cannot be cured, cats with uveitis can be treated symptomatically to ease discomfort and maintain vision. Long-term uveitis can lead to cataract formation, lens luxation and glaucoma. Non-infectious causes of uveitis include trauma and neoplasia.

Atrophy of the iris may occur as a result of ageing or following inflammation. Cysts of the iris are sometimes seen and look like black balloons. They form on the back of the iris but can detach and float through the pupil to rest in front. They are not neoplastic and do not usually need to be removed.

Uveitis, inflammation of the iris, ciliary body and choroid.

LENS

The lens is the clear disc-shaped structure suspended behind the iris, responsible for focusing light onto the retina. A cataract, or opacity of the lens and/or its capsule, is a disorder of the lens. Many forms of hereditary cataract are seen in dogs but not in cats. Congenital cataracts are occasionally found as a non-inherited problem. Most of the cataracts seen in cats are formed secondary to lens damage, e.g. blunt trauma, penetrating wounds, chronic anterior uveitis and lens luxation. If cataracts involve the whole lens, light will not be able to get through to the retina and the eye will be rendered blind. If appropriate, cataracts can be surgically removed.

If the lens's suspensory fibres weaken or break, it will become dislocated and can fall either into the back or front of the eye. This is a common breed-related problem

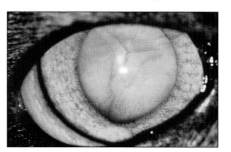

Cataract developed from long-term uveitis.

in terrier dogs and is occasionally seen in cats, usually as a result of trauma, ageing or cataract. The lens is usually surgically removed to prevent it from blocking the pupil, which can lead to glaucoma.

The lens condenses with age, giving it a grey appearance, known as senile sclerosis. This is not a true cataract as light can still pass through to the back of the eye and vision is not impaired.

One rare but important condition of the lens in the cat is post-traumatic sarcoma. If the lens is damaged by trauma, it can become neoplastic and rapidly fill the eye with tumours. Appropriate treatment at the time of the initial injury should prevent this, but when it does occur, surgical removal of the eye is recommended.

VITREOUS HUMOUR

The vitreous humour is a jelly-like substance that fills the space between the back of the lens and the front of the retina. Like the aqueous humour, the vitreous can be infiltrated with haemorrhage and inflammatory cells. Foreign bodies can occasionally be found in the vitreous. Inflammation of the vitreous, known as hyalitis, can be seen as part of generalised uveitis.

The vitreous humour degenerates with age, giving a

> **THINGS TO LOOK OUT FOR**
> A change in appearance of the eye
> * Redness
> * Cloudiness
> * Change in iris colour
> Increase in discharges
> * Watery
> Sticky mucoid
> * Yellow
> * Bloody
> Blinking, squinting and head shyness
> Aversion to light
> Rubbing at the eye
> Loss of vision
> Protrusion of the eye
> Loss of facial symmetry

cloudy appearance to the back of the eye, but this does not usually affect vision to any great extent.

RETINA

The retina, at the back of the eye, is where the visual image is formed. Congenital retinal problems are rare in cats, but colobomas (defects or holes) can occasionally be seen in the optic disc (the point at which nerves converge to leave the eye as the optic nerve). Inflammation of the retina usually occurs together with inflammation of the choroid and is called chorioretinitis or posterior uveitis. The causes are the same as those for anterior uveitis. Inflammation can lead to retinal detachment, haemorrhage, degeneration and scarring of the retina. It can be

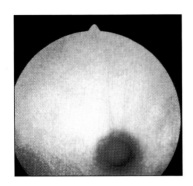

difficult to diagnose the cause of posterior uveitis, thus symptomatic treatment is generally given to maintain vision.

The retina may also degenerate as a result of non-inflammatory processes. An inherited form of retinal degeneration has been described in the Abyssinian and Siamese breeds. Deficiency in dietary taurine (an amino acid) causes retinal degeneration. Fortunately, this is now rare as many commercial cat foods are supplemented with this compound. It may, however, still be a problem with some home-prepared diets.

Hypertension is a common cause of retinal disease in elderly cats. It may be primary, essential hypertension or secondary to other diseases, such as kidney disease, hyperthyroidism and diabetes. Hypertension causes changes in the retinal arteries, retinal and vitreal haemorrhages, retinal detachment and hyphaema. Early recognition and treatment are essential to prevent permanent ocular damage and damage to other organs, such as the kidney, heart and brain.

Retinal detachment causes blindness and may result from hypertension, inflammation and neoplasia. If the retina does not reattach in 24–48 hours, there will be permanent vision loss. Symptomatic treatment is often given to reattach the retina, but it is also important to treat the underlying cause.

Retinal haemorrhages can occur as a result of hypertension, inflammation and trauma. They can cause temporary loss of vision but will often be resorbed. Once again, it is important to find the underlying cause and treat it accordingly without delay.

Finally, if in any doubt regarding the condition of your cat's eyes, it is always worthwhile consulting your veterinary surgeon. Even if you consider the condition minor, it may not remain so!

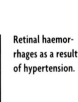

Advanced retinal degeneration.

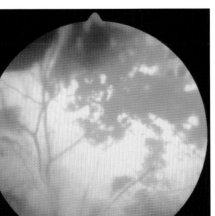

Retinal haemor-rhages as a result of hypertension.

The author is grateful to the Animal Health Trust (England) for the illustrations used in the eye health section.

FIRST AID AT A GLANCE

BURNS/SCALDS
Place the affected area under cool water; use ice if only a small area is burnt. Do not cover the burn or clip hair away. Petroleum jelly can be applied; take cat to vet immediately.

CHEMICAL BURNS
Wash with water only. If you know the chemical is acid, a weak solution of sodium bicarbonate will help, or a vinegar solution will do for alkaline burns.

BEE/INSECT BITES
Apply freshly sliced onion. Apply ice to relieve swelling; antihistamine dosed properly.

AUTOMOBILE ACCIDENT
Move cat from roadway with blanket; seek veterinary aid.

ANIMAL BITES
Clean any bleeding area; apply pressure until bleeding subsides; go to the vet.

SHOCK
Calm the cat, keep him warm and in a horizontal position; seek immediate veterinary aid.

SPIDER BITES
Use cold compress and a pressurised pack to inhibit venom's spreading.

NOSEBLEED
Apply cold compress to the nose; apply pressure to any visible abrasion.

ANTIFREEZE POISONING
Induce vomiting with hydrogen peroxide. Seek *immediate* veterinary help!

BLEEDING
Apply pressure above the area; treat wound by applying a cotton pack.

FISH HOOKS
Removal best handled by vet; hook must be cut in order to remove.

HEAT STROKE
Move animal to cool, shaded area, wet animal with water and place ice packs around head and body; seek immediate veterinary aid.

SNAKE BITES
Pack ice around bite; contact vet quickly; identify snake for proper antivenin.

FROSTBITE/HYPOTHERMIA
Warm the cat with a warm bath, electric blankets or hot water bottles.

ASPHYXIA
Cat must breathe fresh air as soon as possible. Encourage your cat to move around.

ABRASIONS
Clean the wound and wash out thoroughly with fresh water; apply antiseptic.

Remember: an injured cat may attempt to bite a helping hand from fear and confusion. Handle your cat in a calm and gentle manner so as to avoid upsetting the animal further.

Recognising a Sick Cat

Unlike colicky babies and cranky children, our feline charges cannot tell us when they are feeling ill. Therefore, there are a number of signs that owners can identify to know that their cats are not feeling well.

**Take note for
physical manifestations such as:**

- unusual, bad odour, including bad breath
- excessive moulting
- wax in the ears, chronic ear irritation
- oily, flaky, dull haircoat
- mucous, tearing or similar discharge in the eyes
- fleas or mites
- mucous in stool, diarrhoea
- sensitivity to petting or handling
- licking at paws, scratching face, etc.

**Keep an eye out for
behavioural changes as well including:**

- lethargy, idleness
- lack of patience or general irritability
- lack of appetite, digestive problems
- phobias (fear of people, loud noises, etc.)
- strange behaviour, suspicion, fear
- coprophagia
- whimpering, crying

Get Well Soon

You don't need a DVR or a BVMA to provide good TLC to your sick or recovering cat, but you do need to pay attention to some details that normally wouldn't bother him. The following tips will aid Kitty's recovery and get him back on his paws again:

- Keep his space free of irritating smells, like heavy perfumes and air fresheners.
- Rest is the best medicine! Avoid harsh lighting that will prevent your cat from sleeping. Shade him from bright sunlight during the day and dim the lights in the evening.
- Keep the noise level down. Animals are more sensitive to sound when they are sick.

- Be attentive to any necessary temperature adjustments. A cat with a fever needs a cool room and cold liquids. A queen that is birthing or recovering from surgery will be more comfortable in a warm room, consuming warm liquids and food.
- You wouldn't send a sick child back to school early, so don't rush your cat back into a full routine until he seems absolutely ready.

USEFUL ADDRESSES

GREAT BRITAIN
The Governing Council of the Cat Fancy (GCCF)
4-6 Penel Orlieu, Bridgwater, Somerset, TA6 3PG
Email: GCCF_CATS@compuserve.com Fax: 01278 446627 Tel: 01278 427575

The Cat Association of Britain
Mill House, Letcombe Regis, Oxon OX12 9JD   Tel: 01235 766543

EUROPE
Federation Internationale Feline (FIFe)
Gen. Sec: Ms Penelope Bydlinski.
Little Dene, Lenham Heath, Maidstone, Kent ME17 2BS, GB
Email: penbyd@compuserve.com   Fax: 1622 850193 Tel: 1622 850908

World Cat Federation
Hubertsrabe 280, D-45307, Essen, Germany
Email: wcf@nrw-online.de   Fax: 201-552747 Tel: 201-555724

AUSTRALIA
The Australian Cat Federation, Inc.
PO Box 3305, Port Adelaide, SA 5015
Email: acf@catlover.com   Fax: 08 8242 2767 Tel: 08 8449 5880

CANADA
Canadian Cat Association
220 Advance Boulevard, Suite 101, Brampton, Ontario L6T 4J5
Email: office@cca-afc.com   Fax: 99050 459-4023 Tel: 99060 459-1481

SOUTH AFRICA
Cat Federation of Southern Africa
PO Box 25, Bromhof 2154, Gauteng Province, Republic of South Africa

USA
American Cat Association
8101 Katherine Avenue, Panorama City, CA 91402
Fax: (818) 781-5340 Tel: (818) 781-5656

American Cat Fanciers Association
PO Box 203, Point Lookout, MO 65726
Email: info@acfacat.com   Fax: (417) 334-5540 Tel: (417) 334-5430

Cat Fanciers Association, Inc.
PO Box 1005, Manasquan, NJ 08736-0805
Email: cfa@cfainc.org   Fax: (732) 528-7391 Tel: (732) 528-9797

Cat Fanciers Federation
PO Box 661, Gratis, OH 45330
Email: Lalbert933@aol.com Fax: (937) 787-4290 Tel: (937) 787-9009

The International Cat Association
PO Box 2684, Harlingen, TX 78551
Email: ticaeo@xanadu2.net Tel: (956) 428-8046